"I could write a lengthy essay showing why this autobiography in particular is an accurate portrayal of the alcoholic family. The proof, however, lies in the reading. Show this book to *any* child or adult who can read (and whom you might suspect on the flimsiest of evidence to have a problem of alcohol in the family). That child will come back to you and say, 'This is how it is.' And then you and that person can start discussing what the two of you together can do to start healing the pain.

"If you are, like me, the child of an alcoholic, if you identify with most of the characteristics of children of alcoholics listed at the end of this book, if you read *Potato Chips for Breakfast* and said, 'Crissy is me,' then reach out. We're here in the sunlight waiting for you."

—From the Afterword by Thomas W. Perrin, M.A.

Potato Chips For Breakfast
An Autobiography

by

Cynthia G. Scales

BANTAM BOOKS
NEW YORK · TORONTO · LONDON · SYDNEY · AUCKLAND

POTATO CHIPS FOR BREAKFAST

A Bantam Book / published by arrangement with Quotidian

PRINTING HISTORY
Quotidian edition published 1986
Material from WHAT TO DO and COMMON CHARACTERISTICS OF ADULT CHILDREN FROM DYSFUNCTIONAL FAMILIES,
copyright © 1986 by Thomas W. Perrin. Printed by permission.

Bantam edition / July 1989

ISBN 0-553-28166-6

Published simultaneously in the United States and Canada

Bantam Books are published by Bantam Books, a division of Bantam Doubleday Dell Publishing Group, Inc. Its trademark, consisting of the words "Bantam Books" and the portrayal of a rooster, is Registered in U.S. Patent and Trademark Office and in other countries. Marca Registrada. Bantam Books, 666 Fifth Avenue, New York, New York 10103.

PRINTED IN THE UNITED STATES OF AMERICA

O   0 9 8 7 6 5 4 3 2 1

DEDICATED
TO MY PARENTS
AND TO ALL PARENTS WHO STRUGGLE
WITH A DISEASE THEY
DON'T KNOW THEY HAVE

MY THANKS TO THE FOLLOWING SPECIAL PEOPLE:

To Peter and my two sons, Tom and Matt, who encourage and believe in me.

To Jane Thomas who worked over the manuscript.

To Tom Perrin, who cared enough to find QUOTIDIAN.

To Judy Knowlton, the woman who believed and cared enough to publish my story.

AND TO MANY PEOPLE WHO HAVE ENRICHED MY LIFE, HELPING ME TO GET TO HERE FROM THERE:

To my dear friend Bob O'Dell, M.D.

To Mark Held (held by Held).

To Gini Buchtor, who said I must write.

To Paul Sulley, who flies with me and is always willing "to take any plane that's on the runway."

To Aunt Sue, my consummate role model.

To Carolyn Peter and her son, Adam.

To Hazel Cholmondoley, who didn't care what color I was.

To everyone at the Alaska Council on Prevention of Alcohol and Drug Abuse. That includes you, Joyce Schwettman.

To Eloise, wherever you are.

To Marge.

Most of all, to teachers everywhere.

Potato Chips
For
Breakfast

CHAPTER 1

January 21, 1963

Telling the truth means giving away the secret in my family. Everybody lies in my family. It makes my stomach hurt.

I'm fifteen years old. I can't tell if I'm pretty or not. I used to be cute. People told me that. Now they say I'm mature acting for my age. My boobs are too big. My legs are okay. My waist is fat. My dad said I'm built like a brick shithouse. He was mad when he said it. I don't know what a brick shithouse looks like. I imagine it's ugly.

Both my parents are alcoholics. That's a terrible thing to say about your parents. I have a hard time believing it myself. We live in a big house. Mom drives a Cadillac and Eloise cleans the house. Some of my friends call my family rich. I think alcoholics are bums. Poor people that nobody cares about who sleep on the street. Still, I'm pretty sure my parents are alkies.

When I was a little kid I already knew what hangovers were. A hangover was when I couldn't bother my parents. They'd stay in bed. That's when I used to give my baby brother potato chips and Coke for breakfast. Mom's hangovers last forever now.

My little brother is three years younger than I am. He's twelve. He's real nervous and scared all the time. The palms of his hands and the bottoms of his feet itch like crazy. He scratches them till they bleed. He's also tubby. His name is Gordon.

We have a french poodle named Gigi.

My mom is beautiful with long blonde hair. She'd be better-looking if she didn't have a stomach that looks pregnant. Her eyelashes are real weird, too. They grow down over her eyes. She curls them with an eyelash curler, but they go right back down. Her name is Wanda. Wanda the Witch.

They call my dad Big George. He's fat. Not just fat. Huge! He's not as drunk as my mother all the time. I've seen pictures of when he was young. He was very handsome. He goes to work every day. Sometimes I hear him getting mad at the people who work for him. He yells at them on the phone and tells them they're fired. He's the boss.

We live in Farfield Hills, Illinois. Eloise cleans the house on Mondays and Thursdays. She's black and just had her breast taken off because of cancer. She chews tobacco and thinks I don't know it. I love coming home on the days she's here. I come in the door and stand at the top of the basement stairs and yell, "Yoo-hoo, Eloise!"

She yells back, "Yoo-hoo, I's right here!" Then she asks me how my day was. She sits down with me while I have a snack.

My name is Crissy.

CHAPTER 2

February 4, 1963

Today is Tuesday. It's cold. Snowing. Eloise isn't here and the door is locked with a chain on the inside. It's one of those little gold chains. The kitchen door has nine window panes. I'm in the garage. I'm ringing the doorbell, pounding on the door and yelling. There's no answer. When I find the hammer I'm going to break the window and get in. I'm shivering.

Got the hammer. Now the trick is to break the glass without tearing the green curtain. It's not easy to break a window. I hit it three times before it breaks. I hate breaking stuff. I should be used to doing this. It's the fourth time.

Inside cleaning up the glass, I think I should go looking for Mom. Her car is in the garage. I know she's home.

Instead I make some toast with butter and jelly. Used to be I never liked butter. I probably shouldn't like it now. I know it makes me fat.

* * *

I'm in my room waiting for my little brother to get home.

I never think of him by his name. Gordon is a dumb name and he gets mad when I call him Gordie. When he comes in I want him to be quiet.

I know if my mom didn't wake up when I broke the window Gordie probably can't wake her now. It's just there's no sense taking a chance. I like it nice and peaceful.

＊ ＊ ＊

I fell asleep on my bed. It's totally dark. I can hear my dad yelling, "Who broke the window?" I go downstairs to tell him.

"I had to break the window to get in." I watch him pour straight vodka in a tall glass.

"Couldn't you find some other way in?" he asks.

"No. It was chained from the inside," I say as I open the bag of White Tower hamburgers he brought home for dinner. I love White Tower. It's one of my favorite meals.

"Where's your brother?" Dad asks.

I can hear the television in the family room. "He's probably watching TV." I know he is—sitting with his legs curled up under a couple of blankets. He sits right on the end of the couch about ten inches from the TV set. I've told him a hundred times it's bad for his eyes. I tell him he can get radiation from the TV, but he doesn't listen.

"Where's your mother?" Dad asks as he finishes his first glass of vodka.

"Where do you think she is?" I say real nasty.

"Don't get smart with me. I asked where your mother is." He sounds mad.

"She's in the basement, drunk," I say.

"Keep up that fresh mouth and you're gonna get a fat lip," he says as he pours another glass of vodka and puts the bottle back in the freezer.

He looks at me for a minute like he's trying to decide something.

Finally he says, "She can't be drunk. I had a new lock put on the liquor cabinet this morning."

It's better not to argue with him. Besides, if I wait he'll go downstairs and find her passed out.

Gordie gets in on the act. Coming into the kitchen he can smell the hamburgers. "Where's Mom?" he asks.

"She's in the basement." I make a singsong of the words. Everyone acts like nothing's wrong.

Dad heads for the basement. My brother follows him. I wait in the kitchen eating burgers.

The fun is about to begin.

Our house is a colonial. Upstairs it's got four bedrooms, a dressing room and two bathrooms. The stairs are in the middle of the house with a black and white tiled foyer at the bottom. A foyer is a fancy front hall. On one side of the foyer is the living room and on the other side is the dining room. We don't use them much. In the back of the house is the kitchen and the family room. There's a black tiled bathroom and what used to be a storage closet. Now it's got a bar with a sink and small refrigerator. There's also a door leading to the basement.

I walk back there with my third hamburger. My brother is coming up the stairs first. Behind him is my mother. My dad is behind her and it's a good thing because every time she starts to fall he pushes her back upright.

"Wanda, get a hold of yourself and wake up," he snarls at her.

Mom doesn't say anything. My brother speeds by me and grabs a burger.

At the top of the stairs Mom sees me. She says something like, "Hi, honey, how are you?" I can't make out the words exactly because they all run together.

"You're drunk!" My voice is full of hate.

"Leave your mother alone, Crissy. Go to your room if you're going to be nasty." Dad sounds mean.

Mom's bouncing down the hall toward me. She bumps into one wall, bounces off that into the other wall.

"Normal people don't walk into walls. She's drunk. I can smell her!" I yell.

'She's not drunk!" my brother yells from the kitchen.

Before I can yell again, Gordie adds, "She promised me last night she wouldn't drink anymore."

"She's drunk as a skunk!" I scream.

"Crissy, you're crazy. Stop being hysterical or I'll slap you," Dad orders.

"You can call me crazy all you want. When are you guys gonna realize she's a drunk? You're both just pretending that she's not." My face feels hot from yelling and trying not to cry.

"Your mother is on medication from her doctor," says Dad as he tries to grab Mom before she hits the pantry door.

The door groans as she hits it.

"Medicine, my ass! She's drunk. You're the ones that are crazy!"

Dad slaps my face. My hamburger falls on the floor and Gigi eats it.

"Somebody better feed the dog and it didn't hurt when you hit me," I say as I run to my room. My face is stinging.

I can pretty much live in my room without going out. I have my own TV and a telephone with my own number. Except for food I don't ever have to leave my room.

Off and on I hear screaming downstairs. I'm at the point where I can tell if it's serious or not. I can tell if the noise means someone is getting killed. The TV is on in my brother's room so I can tell he's okay.

Homework is something I can't concentrate on. I'm getting C's and D's and flunking algebra. I used to get all A's.

Life's lousy in my house and this wasn't even a bad day.

I sleep a lot more than I used to.

CHAPTER 3

February 13, 1963

I can smell something burning. Dinnertime in my house is a joke.

The kitchen is filled with black smoke. It's pouring out of the oven. I grab a hot pad before I open the door. Refrigerator rolls. Once in a while Mom cooks dinner. The rolls are black. Who cares? It's nine o'clock already. It's too late for dinner anyway.

I hear shouting from the family room.

"You smell like a bar. Don't lie to me. I know you've been drinking, you liar!" Dad yells.

"You bitch! You ugly bitch!" He's attacking her. I can tell.

He's got her by the hair, dragging her through the hall, into the foyer and up the stairs. She's screaming at the top of her lungs. You know what it sounds like? Just like a dog that's been hit by a car!

I run to the family room to check on my brother. He's okay. He's sitting just like he always does in front of the TV. I forget to tell him he's sitting too close.

I run upstairs, two at a time. This may be one of those times that if I don't call the cops or stop the fight, Dad will really kill Mom. I don't want to go up there and find out.

They're in the bathroom. Dad is holding Mom's head in the toilet bowl and yelling, "I'm gonna flush you down the toilet! That's all you're good for, you fucking bitch!"

He's holding her head down in the toilet with one hand and flushing the toilet with the other.

I'm screaming so loud my throat hurts. "Stop it! Stop it! You'll drown her, Dad! Stop it!"

I try to pull my mom out of the toilet.

"If you kill her you'll go to jail!" I'm yelling as loud as I can so he'll pay attention to me. My mom's screaming and the toilet is flushing. I can see her long blonde hair flowing down the hole at the bottom of the toilet bowl.

"Nobody's gonna put me in jail! It's self defense. Look at me! I'm bleeding!" Dad yells back.

His chest is oozing from fingernail scratches. "But you're bigger than she is!" I scream.

The toilet bowl is filling up with water again. In seconds it'll cover her nose and part of her mouth. I stare at it rising.

I turn on my little girl voice. "If you kill her you'll go to jail and we won't have any parents at all." I say this real quiet.

He must feel sorry for me because he throws my mom on the floor and stomps out of the bathroom. I put a towel on her hair and go to my room. Thank God I don't have to call the cops tonight!

I hate it when I call the cops. First, because I shake all over; then, because the cops never do anything. Old Scottie just comes in and says, "Hi, how ya doin', Mr. Mahr. Having a little trouble here? We got a call."

I get in a lot of trouble with my dad for calling the cops.

* * *

When I was a kid I used to think the grossest thing in the world was Carrie Brombeck chewing tuna fish with her mouth open. Now it's my parents.

* * *

There's something I never talk about. It's that I sweat all the time. My arm pits are like a rain forest. I've used every deodorant, even "Secret".

CHAPTER 4

February 14, 1963
Valentine's Day

Getting rid of last night is going to be hard.

My room is blue. Pure, deep sky blue. Blue carpet, blue bedspread, blue walls and blue curtains. There's a white ceiling, but with the curtains closed the light shows everything blue. My bedroom cost a lot of money.

They say colors can have an effect on you. Blue is a sad color, isn't it? All the blue in my room is probably why I feel miserable. Someday I'm going to wake up in a yellow bedroom with white frills and little daisies or pink roses.

First thing this morning, just like every morning, I go downstairs. I fill a tall glass with ice and pour myself a Coke. Coke's good for me. It settles my stomach. I stopped eating potato chips for breakfast. They're fattening.

I take a shower every day. Splashing around in a bathtub is like still being a kid. My bathroom is gray and yellow. Actually all that's yellow is the toilet and the bathtub and the sink.

I step on the gray scale that matches everything. A hundred and twenty four pounds? God, am I fat! Being a teenager has made me fat. I better stop weighing myself twice a day.

This part of my morning takes an hour. I sit on my vanity bench and look in the mirror for pimples. I get them on my chin and forehead. I hate the big ones that are hard and hurt. There's no way to pick them. Today all I can find is a couple of blackheads. It's good to squeeze the blackheads out before they turn to whiteheads.

Sitting under my blue hairdryer reminds me of when I was a little girl. My mother would take me to her hairdresser. The lady would cut my hair in her dining room and then take me out under a big hairdryer in her cozy little den. I'd sit there all alone. She'd bring me a bowl of coffee ice cream. I'd sit there eating it—a million miles from anything. Not even noise to hurt me. All alone. Safe.

That reminds me. In our old neighborhood, before we moved here when I was twelve, there was a lady named Mabel Jones. Her daughter Lynn was my age. I stopped there every morning on the way to school. Mrs. Jones would comb my hair and kiss me goodbye just like Lynn.

She used to say, "I know you get up alone and no one fixes your breakfast. But you should always have a kiss."

I always had to wipe her lipstick off my cheek.

A lot of times she used to make me eat something too. If it was pancakes or french toast I would. I hate eggs and oatmeal. Now I don't eat in the morning. I'm hardly ever hungry that early.

Time to take off the hairdryer and see how my hair came out. If it doesn't come out perfectly in the right places I look terrible.

Sometimes I cut my own hair to make it look just right. I only do that when I feel real ugly. Sometimes it looks worse after I cut it.

I smoke in my room. Marlboros.

It takes a while to put on my makeup. I make it look like I'm not wearing any.

This time I change my outfit three times before I look okay, not too fat. All the clothes I don't wear I pile up on my chaise lounge. Eloise will take care of them.

Perfume is last. Madame Roaches. I have a thing about wearing perfume. When I forget I feel naked. A couple of times I stayed home from school when I missed the bus because I had to go back when I forgot my perfume.

It's cold outside. I choose my polo coat, not my Chesterfield. I stop at Kathy Jenkin's house on the way to the bus. Her mom is fixing her tea and toast. They are fighting about whether she has to eat breakfast. They do that all the time.

Lately Kathy and her mother have been a little mad at me. I sent Kathy's picture into Mad magazine and they put it in the pen pal section. She's been getting weird letters from all over the U.S.A.

I remember Mom and I fighting once before school. I don't remember what I did. I probably talked back or got hysterical. Mom stuck my head under the faucet in the kitchen sink. She turned on freezing cold water and got my hair wet. She made me go to school that way. I was eight years old.

* * *

I don't think I'm as popular as I used to be. Freshman year I was Treasurer of my class. This year I ran for Student Council. Someone told me that my guidance counselor said it might keep me out of trouble. He put my name up. I didn't get elected.

I walk down the hall and never say hi to anybody unless they say hi to me first. I can't stand it when you say hi to somebody and they just walk by like they don't know you. There are about seventeen hundred kids in my school.

Algebra is the class I hate the most. Some of my classes I can sleep through. My algebra teacher is a witch. She caught me cheating once. Now I have to sit in the front.

The guy who sits next to me is a junior. He's always knocking my books on the floor. His name is Craig.

Today the teacher is walking around passing out a quiz when Craig reaches over and knocks my books on the floor.

This time it gets to me. I jump up, run around to the back of his desk and push it over. With him in it! He's a pretty big guy.

When he tries to get up I hit him on the head with a book. I hit him again and again. I don't care if I bash his skull to pieces!

Everybody sits there like they can't believe what's happening. Mostly I talk quiet and act real shy. People keep telling me to speak up so they can hear me. This better teach Craig to stop teasing me.

My algebra teacher sends me to the office. I sit in the principal's office waiting to see Mr. Burgess. He's the assistant principal.

I never used to get into trouble in school. When I was little I was teacher's pet. All my grade school teachers gave me hugs and special chores to help them.

Life changed in Junior High. I changed teachers every hour. None of them ever gave me a special feeling or started to like me. Now the only one who's really nice to me is Mr. Burgess, and I only see him when I'm in trouble.

"Crissy, come in here," says Mr. Burgess. He's letting my algebra teacher out of his office.

I go slow into his office. It's a little office without any windows. Mr. Burgess is the guy everybody sees when they get in trouble. I've been here before. Once for skipping school.

He points me to a chair. He leans forward so his face is only a few inches from mine. I want to sit further away, but I can't.

"Crissy, why did you start a fight with Craig?" he asks softly.

"I don't know. I really don't." I am telling the truth.

"Come on, Crissy, think about why you were so angry," he says.

"I was just mad." I think for the first time that maybe I <u>was</u> mad.

"Mad about what?" he asks.

"Because Craig threw my books on the floor," I tell him.

"From what I hear you were madder than most people get if someone threw their books on the floor. You could have hurt Craig," says Mr. Burgess seriously.

"He's a lot bigger than me. He could've hurt me a lot worse," I say back.

"That's true. He could have. He didn't hit back because you're a girl," he says.

"That's a lie. He was scared to hit me in front of everyone," I argue.

"Crissy, I've had lots of kids in my office for fighting— boys fighting boys—girls fighting girls—but this is the first time I've had a girl start a fight with a boy," he says.

"He started it!" I remind him.

"Crissy, I'm going to suspend you for three days." He waits for me to react. I don't move at all.

He starts to talk first. "I know your parents. I know they aren't going to do anything. I know how it is in your family."

I don't tell him what happened in my family last night. I just wait to see what he's going to do next.

"Because I know you'll be home without any supervision, I'm giving you thirty pages of algebra problems to do. That's ten pages a day. I won't let you back into school until they are done."

I want to ask who's going to correct the papers. I figure I can put any old answer down. He didn't say they had to be right.

He's still talking: "...so that's twice a day I'm going to call you. When school starts in the morning and when it's over at three fifteen. You'll have to get up and work on the problems."

"Do you understand?" he asks.

"Yes," I whisper.

Mr. Burgess is a nice guy. One day he told me how his little boy died. Leukemia killed him. He said that at first he and his wife thought the bruises on his son's legs were nothing but "little kids' bruises" from riding his bike.

I know Mr. Burgess cares about me. He ends our conversation by saying he hates to do this to me and he doesn't know if it will help.

Actually, staying home from school for three days won't be too bad. I'll tell Dad I'm sick. Mom will never notice I'm home.

Happy Valentine's Day!

CHAPTER 5

February 18, 1963

Mr. Burgess called twice a day. Just like he said he would. I did all the algebra problems right. Mom and Dad didn't bug me. Maybe they thought I was really sick. I never got out of bed much.

Tonight, Dad and Mom are fighting. What's new?

I'm in my room when Dad yells for me to get the keys to Mom's car. Her car is a green Cadillac convertible. Everything in it is automatic—power seats, power windows and antenna. Everything. It's a big car, and fast. One little touch of the steering wheel and the car takes off in that direction.

It's already dark out. Dad yells at me again, "Get the keys, Crissy. Now!"

I figure he wants me to get the keys so he can hide them. Dad does that a lot. He stops Mom from drunk driving. Sometimes he does it to stop her from getting more liquor. Once the cops picked her up for running off the side of the road. She was on her way to the dump with two big trash bags full of empty booze bottles. She didn't get a ticket after Dad talked to the cops. Dad told me about it.

I go downstairs to look for the car keys on the keyboard my brother made at school. After finding them, I don't want to go back upstairs. I hate going into their bedroom. It smells bad. Both my parents' bodies stink. It's on the sheets and fills the room. The smell is almost too sickening. Like a mixture of old beer, dirty diapers and rotten tennis shoes.

I'm trying to decide what to do with the keys so I don't have to go in there. I hear them coming out.

Dad is dragging Mom down the stairs by her shoulders. She's yelling at him to stop. I stand in the foyer watching. Dad is pulling her down the stairs backwards. Her hands are hooked together behind her back with silver handcuffs. Her feet never land on the stairs. Every few steps Dad stops to rest and her legs hit the stairs straight up in front of her. She's facing upstairs.

"George, you're hurting me. Stop it!" screeches Mom.

"Shut up you slut! You bitch! You whore!" yells Dad.

I don't want to be here.

"Crissy, go start the car," Dad orders me.

"Where are you going?" I ask.

"We are taking your mother to the hospital. The loony bin. We're going to dry her out—get the booze out of her system." He makes every word mean.

I see the pistol stuck in his belt.

Mom is screaming again at the top of her lungs. Not words—long howls. That broken-dog sound.

I check on my brother. He's asleep in his room with the TV going.

Dad takes the pistol and points it against her forehead. He clicks the safety off. Mom shuts up.

My dad is an expert on guns. He collects them. He taught me to shoot skeet and trap at the Illinois Gun Club.

I'm standing here like I'm frozen.

"Crissy, get going. You're driving!" yells Big George.

"I can't drive," I plead. "I don't know how."

"You WILL drive. I'll keep your mother under control," Dad orders me.

I'm worried he'll shoot the gun.

I drive sitting alone in the front seat. Dad holds the gun on Mom's head in the back seat. I keep hoping a cop will stop us. If you don't know how to drive and your dad is in the back seat with a loaded gun and your mom is handcuffed—believe me, it's bad. I'm worried that I won't be able to keep the car in between the white lines.

"Speed up! You're driving too slow! This is a sixty-five mile speed limit!" yells my dad.

Every time the screaming starts in the back seat, I turn around to see if Dad's going to shoot Mom. The car keeps getting off on the side of the road. Trucks go by so fast the car is shaking.

At the hospital, I hope I can park the car. I sweat so much my blouse is soaking wet. I'm wet all the way down to the top of my white pants. It's embarrassing to sweat so much for a girl.

Dad takes the handcuffs off Mom. He puts them in the glove box with the gun. He shoves her toward the hospital entrance. It takes me a few minutes to get my legs to stop shaking enough to follow them.

* * *

The hospital is bright. The light hurts my eyes. A man in a suit and tie tells me that Dad is checking Mom in and points me to a waiting room. A couple of nuns in black robes are walking through the lobby. Everyone seems very far away to me.

I pretend I'm reading a magazine. I can't even concentrate on the picture. I think I'm the one that should be in the hospital.

I had my appendix out here last Spring. I liked it, except for the pain. A nurse said goodnight to me every single night. My parents didn't come to visit much. One time they did, the nurse made them go outside when they started a fight in my room. I spent the time eating three meals a day and watching funny old movies. My stitches hurt because I laughed so much.

No one seems to notice me in this hospital. I have this

strange urge to start yelling about how I had to drive here. I'd like to see my dad get arrested for making me do it.

* * *

It takes a long time to check Mom in. When Dad comes to get me I can tell he's still mad. He's keeping it under control with people around.

On the way home he keeps talking about some lousy law. Mom can get out of the hospital in seventy-two hours if she doesn't want to stay on her own free will. He says he'll see what his lawyer can do about it. He says he'll have mom declared legally insane if he has to. He says he wants Mom to get well.

* * *

Mom is in the hospital for three weeks. I hope when she gets out she's cured.

I'm reading a couple of alcohol pamphlets I took out of the hospital. One of them says that alcoholics won't stop drinking until they <u>hit bottom.</u> It says <u>bottom</u> is different for everyone. Sometimes they lose all their money and family. One of the pamphlets says it's a disease. It makes it sound like alcoholics can't help getting drunk. I think all they have to do is stop drinking. It's that simple.

The days Mom is gone are pretty good. Dad sits in his green recliner chair and drinks a fifth of vodka every night. Vodka doesn't smell as bad as scotch. Mom drinks scotch. Dad is relaxed.

* * *

One time we all go to visit Mom in the hospital. There are other families there too. They give a talk about how wonderful the hospital is and show us around. Dad says it's like a country club. No one talks about why Mom is here. Gordie wants to know if they let Mom outside. She says they do.

March 5, 1963

Mom is home from the hospital. She doesn't drink. One day she comes into my room and shows me a card. It's something called "The Twelve Steps". The first one says she's powerless over alcohol. I believe that! It's number three that bothers me. It talks about a Higher Power. God. She can believe in God if she wants to. I know the truth. There is no God.

Everything proves it. Mom starts to drink again about two weeks later. Two ladies from Alcoholics Anonymous come to the house a couple of times. Mom is so drunk they go away. Plus, Dad doesn't like them hanging around.

I can tell there is no God. I learned that the night I had to drive to the hospital. I used to tell Him to make my parents stop fighting and drinking. A God wouldn't let people be like this.

I write the most beautiful poem I ever wrote about how there is no God and then I burn it, both pages.

It's a Friday night when I burn the poem. My parents are going to take me to a movie. They're making me go. I never want to go anywhere with them. They're always embarrassing me in public.

After the poem I take twenty-two aspirin. That's how many there are in the bottle. I don't know if it's enough to kill me. I hope so. I light a match to the poem. I watch it burn and wait to see if the aspirin will make me die.

The aspirin still isn't working when I go to the movie. I wait until we're all sitting in the movie theater. Then I tell them. I tell them I want to die rather than be with them.

Dad jerks us all out of the movie. He drives home fast. Then he makes me drink castor oil and some other awful stuff. I throw up in the bathtub for a long time.

* * *

The next day Dad won't let me out of his sight. My ears are ringing so bad I can hardly hear anything except that.

CHAPTER 6

April 4, 1963

I'm almost sixteen. I think life will get a lot better when I get my driver's license. Also, I'm getting too scared to ride in the car with my mom driving anymore. She's always running off the road. She smashed my brother's bike in the driveway three times. Dad just keeps buying him a new bike.

Susan, my girlfriend, is coming over to spend the night on Friday so we can go to driver's training together. I hope my parents act all right. Most of the time I stay at her house. Her family is okay. Susan is staying here because it's closer to walk to driver's training.

Susan is coming straight home from school with me. The bus driver tries to hassle us about letting Susan ride on my bus, but she doesn't say much. She's afraid she'll get into trouble like she did when my grandma died.

That day I got a note at school saying to take another bus to my aunt Martha's house because something is wrong at home. The other bus driver won't let me ride. She goes and gets <u>my</u> bus driver. They make me get on my own bus.

I start crying and saying my grandmother died. I don't know how I know that. I just do. I must have ESP or something.

They drop me off at my regular bus stop. They don't feel sorry for me. Mrs. McNaughton sees me walking through her backyard to my house. She runs out and tells me I have to go to my aunt's. I don't tell her I think I know what's wrong. She doesn't tell me anything either. She drives me to my aunt's house.

Aunt Martha takes me in her bedroom alone and tells me Grandma is dead. I start crying. All I can think of is her empty chair at Thanksgiving. Will we leave a chair for her next Thanksgiving?

Anyway, Big George makes a big deal about the bus driver's not letting me ride the other bus. Now they never bother me.

* * *

Today I tell Susan about my grandma dying and the bus drivers. I can tell Susan anything, except about my parents' drinking. I know she knows 'cause she's seen them drunk.

There are some kids in my class whose parents won't let them come over to my house because my parents are drunks. Susan's parents aren't like that. I get jealous of her having great parents. I get treated like there's something wrong with me or I'm a bad kid—just because my mom and dad are alcoholics.

Tonight I'm hoping things won't be too bad at my house.

Susan and I let ourselves into the kitchen. I'm lucky the

door isn't chained. Right away I can tell that Mom's passed out in the basement. I can feel it. I tell Susan to check out the fridge for something to eat while I peek in the basement to see if she's really there.

The basement has four rooms and a fruit cellar. There's a furnace room, a huge laundry room with two freezers, a big table for my brother's model train and jig saw. And there's Dad's pistol range. That's where Eloise does the laundry and ironing. There's a bathroom next to the gun closet. The other big room is where Mom's passed out. It's called an entertainment room. It has a real, old fashioned juke box, a bar with a sink, a pool table and couches and chairs around a TV. Mom's on the couch dead drunk. She's snoring like a sick pig. She stinks.

I turn the bell off on my phone so it won't wake her. I have my own private line. One extension is down here and the other is in my bedroom. This way I don't have to run all the way from the basement to the second floor. Sometimes if I'm on the first floor, I have to decide whether to run up or down. The bad part is my little brother can listen in on the other extension.

Gigi has made a mess in the middle of the carpet. I think Mom didn't let her out all day. It's not fair to get mad at the dog when nobody lets her out.

Finding Mom drunk is exactly what I was hoping wouldn't happen. I told her. I told her Susan was spending the night and I didn't want her to get drunk. She promised me.

I don't clean up the dog mess. Mom has to do it.

It seems like all this drinking got worse after Grandma

died. She was my mom's mom. My grandfather called
Mom and said she'd killed her mother. He said it was
because of Mom's problems. After that, Mom hasn't been
the same. She got drunk a lot before that. Now she's drunk
all the time.

Susan and I decide to make some fudge. We do love fudge.
We worry about getting fat, but if we eat nothing but
fudge it's not too bad.

Gordie keeps coming into the kitchen asking when it'll be
finished.

Dad walks in just as the fudge reaches the hardball stage.
That's when we have to get it into the pan fast.

Dad bought barbequed spareribs for dinner.

Susan goes to the bathroom when Dad asks where Mom
is.

I tell him about the dog dirt in the basement. He unlocks
the bar and gets a fifth of vodka. I wonder how long it will
be before Mom finds a way into the liquor closet.

Dad says something about not being able to figure out
where she gets the booze. He took her car keys away last
night.

I almost tell him she gets it delivered. I know because the
guy from the liquor store is here on days I'm home sick
from school.

I don't tell because I never know when he's going to accuse
me of being a smartmouth.

Susan's still in the bathroom and the fudge is getting hard in the pot.

"Dad, please don't get drunk tonight," I plead with him. "Please, Dad. Mom's passed out already, and Susan's going to be here tonight. I can't stand it if you both get drunk." I'm whispering so Susan can't hear.

"Leave me alone," he says. "It's none of your goddamn business what I do. Besides, I'm not an alkie. Your mother is."

"I'm not gonna let you drink." I sound firm.

"Oh no? Ya gonna stop me?" He's ready for a fight.

I put myself in front of the kitchen freezer. I'm in his way to get ice cubes.

He shoves me.

"You're not drinking. I'm not gonna let you," I repeat.

"Try and stop me!" He swings his hips. He acts like he's enjoying this.

"I WILL stop you," I say louder.

"How?" he asks as he pours a tall glass of vodka without the ice cubes.

"Here's how. I'll drink it myself!" I almost spit at him.

I pick up the glass. It tastes awful. It burns like mad.

Dad is laughing at me. He pours another one. I grab it. My whole body shivers with each swallow. This isn't funny. I can't breathe!

Dad pours another. I can't drink anymore. I dump it down the sink. There's no way I can make him stop!

Dad's calling me a fool.

Susan comes out of the bathroom. She can tell there's a fight in the kitchen so she goes and sits in the living room. I follow her. I sit down next to her. We're talking just fine.

All of a sudden everything in the world seems so funny I start laughing. I'm laughing hard, crying and rolling on the floor under one of the tables, all at once. Susan is not laughing. She seems to have lost her sense of humor.

Dad and Susan pick me up off the carpet and drag me into the black bathroom.

I'm sitting on the pink fluffy rug and looking at myself in the full-length mirror. I'm smiling at myself and talking to me.

I can hear loud music coming from somewhere. Next door, I think. I want to go to the party. I don't think I can walk, though.

I don't know how long it is before I start throwing up. I puke for a long time. I start crying I feel so awful. I am really sick.

Susan helps me get to my bed. That's nice. This is the

worst feeling I've ever had in my whole life. Why do my parents drink to feel like this?

* * *

In the middle of the night Susan is screaming. She wakes me up. She turns on the light beside my bed. There are bloody bones in her hair! I start to yell too until I see it's only barbequed spareribs. Gigi must have gotten them off the kitchen table and buried them in the bed. Susan has long, blonde hair. She doesn't think it's at all funny.

That's the way she is, sometimes.

* * *

Saturday. The start of driver's training. I feel like I've been living in a garbage can. My head hurts. I think I might throw up again. Susan and I have Coke for breakfast. My stomach feels better. I'm going to try to go to driver's training. We don't talk about last night. I can't tell if she's mad at me. She washed her hair three times.

I make it through driver's training.

Dad never mentions my drinking. I don't think Mom knows. My brother starts teasing me about it. I punch him in the stomach.

I don't know if Susan will ever want to sleep over at my house again.

CHAPTER 7

May 17, 1963

I have to keep this English journal. We're supposed to write three pages a week about our lives. I can't think of anything to write about.

School will be out for the summer in a couple of weeks. I get sad thinking about what summer used to be. When I was little...

I loved summer time. We had a cottage on Strawberry Lake. All my best memories in the world are there. I was kind of like a girl "Huck Finn". I was free. It was the fun time of my life.

Every day, Dad would drive all the way to the city to work. He'd leave before I got up. Then I'd take a towel and go out to the end of the dock. I'd just lay there and let the sun warm me when it came up. The lake would be flat without a ripple.

About nine or ten o'clock the motor boats would start. The rest of the day the lake would buzz with hydroplanes, outboards, waterskiers, choppy waves.

We had the only inboard motorboat on the lake. It was a

wooden Chris Craft. It was beautiful. I was twelve when I hit another boat with the Chris Craft. The other boat sank. It was fiberglass.

I didn't know the other boat sank. The boat left very fast so it would be closer to the shore when it sank.

My friends and I went back to our cottage. I docked the Chris Craft and we took out the canoe.

When I saw the cops on the dock I got the feeling the other boat was wrecked. I said I was sorry. Dad said, "Insurance will pay for everything." The cops said, "Okay." My parents never said anything to me about it.

Sometimes it's like I don't have parents.

A whole gang of kids hung around together at Strawberry Lake. Most of them lived there all year. One other guy, Eddie, and Gordie and me were the only summer kids.

We did all kinds of stuff. One summer we wrote a newspaper and sold it. One time we had a big circus. At night we built bonfires on the flats and roasted hot dogs. It was always one big party. Our parents drank beer.

Mom never bothered me at the lake. Except once when she found Gordie and me playing with matches near some gasoline cans. She hit us with flyswatters. One of them broke on my brother's butt. We were laughing. Then she held our hands and burned them with matches.

Dad would bring home corn on the cob, warm cinnamon bread, and gladiolas for Mom.

I used to fish with worms I found myself. I caught a big old box turtle two summers in a row. I think it was the same turtle.

Strawberry Lake was the kind of place where you could step in warm dogdoo and not get mad.

* * *

There was a raft on the lake with a diving board. We kids swam all day. After dinner we'd buy candy and pop and take it up to the sandpit. We were always building a fort. That's where I started to smoke.

I stole Mom's cigarettes. I thought she didn't know, but one day she walked into my room when I was twelve. She handed me a cigarette, matches and an ashtray. The ashtray was dirty. She said she knew I was smoking. I've been doing it ever since. I'll never let my kids smoke.

* * *

One summer Barb Minelli and I walked into the woods behind the sandpit. We got lost. We ended up in the swamp and thought we'd die. The grass was over our heads. Our legs were getting cut up. Barb got stung by bees and started to cry because we were dying. I got her up on my shoulders to see if she could figure out where we were. She saw a telephone line. We followed it until we could hear boats. I was hoping we wouldn't die because I wasn't sure very many people would come to my funeral.

We came out of the swamp by the river and then followed

the river to our lake. It was pretty dark when we got home.

I thought my parents would be glad to see me because I was alive. Instead they got mad and grounded me. I had a date that night for the drive-in movie. I liked my date and I loved necking so I hated to miss it.

* * *

I had my first kiss at Strawberry Lake. Bob Grayson did it at the movies. I don't remember what was playing. My legs shook so much I thought I'd never walk again. I wanted to go all the way, but Bob said I was too young. He was seventeen and I was thirteen.

* * *

We never went back to the lake after the summer I was thirteen. My grandfather is selling the place. He owns it, even though we were the only ones who used it. My grandfather says there's too much drinking. He decided to sell it right after Mom started a fire in the cottage. There was a lot of smoke damage.

Just thinking about life without Strawberry Lake makes me want to cry.

* * *

Now we stay home all summer. I hate it. It gets so hot that the kickstand on my bike melts into the road tar.

Things are so bad at home now that I'm making up my

own life for my journal. My English teacher will love reading this. I make up all the things that happen in my house. Like all the nice suppers we have and how we like making popcorn and watching TV together. Tonight I'm going to write about how we all took a bike ride together after dinner.

CHAPTER 8

May 18, 1963

I did something I feel bad about. I didn't mean to do it. I was goofing around in the gym. I tell a bunch of girls in the locker room to watch me. They all stand around while I take off my tennis shoe and hit the fire alarm. The shoe is soft. It doesn't break the alarm the first time—or the second. I think it's funny to show everyone that you can't start the alarm. The third time I hit it, it goes off. I'm as surprised as everyone else!

The whole school goes outside and the fire department comes. I don't tell anyone I did it. I hope no one tells on me. It's weird to see so much commotion over something I did.

* * *

Now I'm lying on my bed. My own phone is ringing.

"Crissy, this is Miss Keane," my gym teacher says when I answer.

"Hi," I say. I bet she knows I set off the alarm.

"Some of the girls say you hit the alarm. Did you?" Miss Keane sounds nice, not mad or anything.

I can't deny it. "Yes," I say.

"Crissy, I hate to do this, but I'm going to have to tell the principal." She still sounds nice.

I don't say anything.

"It would be better if you came to see the principal with me. Will you?" asks Miss Keane.

"Do I have to?" I ask, trying to think of a way I'll never have to go back to school, ever.

"Yes, I think you have to. Crissy, I know you're a nice girl. Tell me why you did it?"

I tell her about how I'd been hitting it. I never thought it would break. She keeps asking more questions. Finally I say I think I did it for attention. She seems to think this is the right answer because she stops asking questions.

I agree to meet her outside the principal's office in the morning.

"Crissy, one more thing," she says before hanging up.

"Yeah?"

"Well, I don't see any reason why you have to tell your parents about this right now," she says.

"Okay." I hadn't planned on telling them.

CHAPTER 9

May 19, 1963

This morning it's hard to get up. I've tried to think of ways to get out of this trouble.

Miss Keane is waiting for me. Instead of going to Mr. Burgess' office, we go straight into the head principal's office. Mr. Burgess is already there with a man who looks like a cop.

Are they going to arrest me? Turning in a false alarm is a CRIME.

"Crissy, you know Mr. Crowley, the principal, and this is Fire Chief Hagen," says Mr. Burgess.

They already know what I did. Miss Keane must've talked to them last night.

Mr. Crowley starts telling me what a serious thing it is to set off the fire alarm. He talks about how long I can go to jail for. He talks about how much of a fine I can pay.

The Fire Chief talks about how much money it costs the taxpayers every time an alarm goes off.

I can't believe it costs five thousand bucks for one false alarm. I wonder what a real fire costs!

Mr. Burgess starts talking next. "Crissy, normally we'd ask your parents here, but we've decided not to."

I don't ask him why.

He goes on, "We think you did this for attention. We think you did it because your home life is so bad right now."

Well, he's right. Home is bad.

"Therefore, we've decided not to tell your parents. We don't want to make things worse for you at home." Mr. Burgess is talking; Mr. Crowley is nodding his head.

The Fire Chief says he knows my parents too.

Sure, he does. I've called the fire department lots. Once when Mom fell asleep with a cigarette and the mattress was on fire. Another time I called the rescue squad when Dad hit Mom so hard he knocked her out. I couldn't wake her up.

There are lots of other times I called.

"We are going to suspend you for five days," says Mr. Crowley.

"This is going to be a different kind of suspension," adds Mr. Burgess.

I'm happy they aren't going to arrest me. Who cares if they suspend me?

"During the suspension—which starts today—you'll come to school on your regular bus. But you are to report to me each morning. I'm going to put you in study hall all day. If you miss a single day you'll be expelled for good. That means you'll never come back to school." Mr. Burgess is doing all the talking. "This is your last chance, Crissy. Any more trouble and you'll be expelled. Do you understand?" he asks.

"Yes," I answer.

Then I add, "I'm sorry. I really didn't mean to cause all this trouble."

Nobody says anything. Finally Mr. Crowley says, "We're sure you didn't realize what you were doing." Then he says he hopes I never have to be in this position again.

"Yes, we hope you've learned a lesson from this. No one wants to be too tough. We do understand what you're going through," says Mr. Burgess.

* * *

I go to room 203 for study hall. I'm sweating so much I'm cold and shaky.

I wish they'd find another place for me to live. I wish my parents would die.

I put my head down in my arms on the desk. The study hall teacher says I'm not allowed to sleep.

I guess it's a good thing they decided not to tell my parents. Sometimes Dad hits me with a riding crop. Usually he just threatens. I never know how they're going to react. Sometimes they get mad. Other times they don't do anything at all.

Sometimes they do strange things, like the time I let my brother's helium balloon go. Gordie starting crying. My mom washed my mouth out with soap for doing it.

What does letting Gordie's balloon go have to do with washing my mouth out with soap? I think I was six.

At least this summer I'll have my driver's permit. Then I won't have to ride with my parents any more. Their driving isn't safe.

Mom has absolutely promised that the first day I'm off from school she'll take me to get my driver's permit. I can't wait.

CHAPTER 10

June 25, 1963

I'm excited. I'm getting my driver's permit!

All I have to do is get Mom to take me to the Licensing Bureau. After we get there, I get my permit. Same thing as a driver's license, I think. I'm going to drive with it just like a real license.

I wanted to get my permit the day school was out. We waited until today because it's the first day Mom feels well enough to take me.

Gordie wants to come with us. I'm hoping Mom will act okay and not flirt with the men. I don't want my little brother to go. It's one more person who can embarrass me. He can say some pretty dumb stuff.

Still, I'm happy to be going!

* * *

There's a line when we get to the Motor Vehicle Department. We have to wait to get forms. I see a couple of other kids my age. They are both guys.

Finally I get up to the window, and the lady asks me for my birth certificate.

I don't have it. Mom doesn't have it. She tells everyone that I am who I say I am and I was born when I said I was.

I can feel my face turning red.

We finally get Mom to leave. She tells everyone in the place that we'll be right back with my birth certificate. I know we won't be back today.

I'm mad at myself for not knowing I need it. Maybe they told me in driver's training. I don't remember.

The drive home is gloomy.

We're going down Diamond toward Beakman. I should be driving. If I'd remembered to bring my birth certificate, I'd be driving.

Mom is curving down Diamond. She isn't in great shape.

She's hitting the gravel on the side of the road, because she can't stay inside the curves. I can see the stop sign coming up at Beakman. I can see a gasoline tanker truck speeding down Beakman. He has no stop sign. I can tell Mom isn't gonna stop at our stop sign. I know the truck is going to run us over.

I watch the truck. It's a silver tanker gas truck. I cover my head. I can't bear to watch it hit us. I know we'll die.

My life is not flashing in front of me. I think we're going to make it. I can see the curb next to me. We made it!

"Thank God!" I'm thinking as the truck hits us. It hits us in the back end. I grab the dash board. It's happening so fast I'm still thanking God. The car is spinning 'round and 'round. When it stops, I'm blind. I can't see anything. I'm blind! I can't see!

"I'm blind!" I scream.

"No you are <u>not.</u> You're okay. It's blood running down your face!" yells Mom.

I wipe the warm gush away from my eyes. I'm not blind. My mother is shouting that we must shut the car off. The key won't turn. The windshield is smashed.

"The car will catch on fire!" yells Mom.

The doors won't open in the front seat. I look for my brother. He's out of the car, kneeling on the ground, holding his stomach. The door he was thrown out of is open. He's quite a ways away from us.

I tell my mother we'd better climb out the back.

I look at the windshield. There's a lot of hair in the broken glass.

There are people around. They help us out. They make me lie down. A man is talking to me, holding my hand. I can see the truck like a toy lying on its side down the road. I wonder if the driver is okay.

* * *

An ambulance brings us to the hospital. Mom, Gordie and I are all on stretchers waiting for X-rays. My brother has no big cuts, but he hurts. The doctors put my head in an ace bandage. Mom's head is all wrapped up too.

I can't remember much about the ambulance ride. I don't feel pain, but I'm scared what my face looks like.

I see Dad walking down the hall toward us. The look on his face is terrible. It must be awful to see your whole family lying in a hospital after a car wreck. His face is white and there's sweat on his forehead. He keeps walking from one stretcher to the other.

I think my clothes are ruined by the blood. Dad says they are waiting for a plastic surgeon to operate on my face. The lower part of my face is okay, Dad says. Mom needs plastic surgery too.

They X-ray my head and take me into an operating room. The doctor is nice. He says they can't put me to sleep, something about head injuries. I have to stay awake and listen to the whole thing. It doesn't hurt that much, but I can feel needle stings and pressure. The doctor says he keeps finding glass in my face. He sews up my leg. I didn't know my leg was cut.

After it's over, I want to know how many stitches he put in. There are too many to count, he says. Hundreds of stitches and I'll need more operations on my forehead. He says my eye will look good. He did most of the stitches in my eyebrow.

June 28, 1963

We've been in the hospital for three days now. My brother has some kind of damage to his kidneys. He's bleeding inside. The doctor sewed up Mom's head and she won't need any more surgery. They're going to let Mom and me go home from the hospital today.

I don't want to leave; I like it here. My friends have been coming in to visit. I tell the doctor I don't think I should go home yet. I'm still dizzy. They are making us go, anyway. They are making a mistake; I'm better off here with someone to take care of me!

The nurse comes in to tell me to get dressed. I'm mad about being sent home. I don't want to leave my brother here alone. I get up off the bed and pretend to faint. I'm careful to fall back on the bed. I can't tell if the nurse knows I'm faking. She goes to find a doctor.

The nurse comes back in and says that I can stay another night, but tomorrow I must go home.

* * *

Everyone, including a policeman, has been asking me about the accident. Dad tells me what I have to say. I'm supposed to say that Mom stopped at the stop sign. It's a lie. Dad says if I don't say that, there could be a lot of trouble. Someone tells me that the poor guy driving the truck had his legs crushed and ribs broken. He'll be in the hospital for a long time.

It bothers me to lie. Dad says it won't hurt anyone; insurance will pay for everything.

Once I've told the lie of Mom stopping at the sign a few times, it's like telling the truth. The truck was speeding. Mom didn't stop, but I tell people she did. My brother is telling the same lie. Mom says she stopped and didn't realize how fast the truck was going. She says she thought she could make it. I don't know what will happen with this lie.

The car is totalled. So is the truck. I guess we're lucky to be alive.

* * *

My head still has a big bandage on it. I haven't been able to see what my forehead looks like. I can lift the bottom of the bandage a little. All I can see is black dried up blood and stitches. I hope my forehead won't look like this forever.

I still ache everywhere. This is all my fault. If I'd remembered my birth certificate there never would have been an accident.

Why do I have this feeling that something bad is going to happen all the time?

CHAPTER 11

October 10, 1963

I'm sixteen. My birthday was September tenth. Sweet sixteen. I've got my driver's license; I'm a junior this year.

The summer was a waste. I never wanted to go anywhere. Everyone stares at the bandage on my head. Some friends come over to my house; Susan washes my hair every three days. I want to wash it every day, but I can't get the bandage wet.

The doctor takes the big ace bandage off my head the week before school starts. I have a smaller one now that covers just my forehead. I cut my hair in bangs to cover it over. It's not so bad, even though it still shows. I feel ugly and fat.

The next operation is going to be around Halloween. After that I'll be able to tell what my forehead looks like. The doctor keeps telling me I'll look great. He says I'll never have wrinkles on my forehead when I get old. That's because he pulled the skin so tight. All my friends say I look pretty. They're just being nice. I can tell.

My brother is okay.

My mom and dad still drink and fight all the time. I had to call the rescue squad once this summer when Mom had convulsions. That's what alcoholics get when they don't get enough booze. Dad handcuffed Mom to the toilet bowl in the bathroom. She drank a bottle of Chanel Number Five. There wasn't enough alcohol in the perfume so she got a convulsion. I've been reading a medical book. Some alcoholics get the DT's and think that snakes are crawling all over them.

Right after Dad let her out of the handcuffs she walked into my room. Mom has a cigarette in her hand when the convulsion happens. All of a sudden she flies backwards. She falls on the floor and jerks all over. It's a good thing I'm there. Otherwise her cigarette might have started a fire in the carpet.

I wonder how long it will be until something really terrible happens.

The days that Eloise comes to clean the house are the only half-way good days at my house.

I've figured out that I'll never be normal. No one can live like this and not go crazy. Dad says my biggest problem is that I think too much.

I beg Dad to send me away to boarding school. He won't. He can afford it. I can't wait to leave home after I graduate next year. No one in my family talks about me going to college like my friends. My grandfather says, "Boys go to college and girls get married." He is very old fashioned.

I haven't met anyone who wants to marry me, yet.

A couple of guys from school came around this summer. One is a real nice guy who wants to be a dentist. They stop coming after Big George comes downstairs one day. We're in the entertainment room. For no reason, he grabs the guys by the neck and drags them upstairs. He throws them out the front door without their shoes. We aren't doing anything wrong. I think Dad asked Gordie what they are doing here and Gordie said, "Screwing around with my sister."

* * *

I did get my driver's license. I'm in a carpool this year with four other girls. We each drive once a week. Today is my turn.

I'm up early. The keys aren't on the board. I have to go into my parents' stinking room to look in Mom's purse. Dad is in the shower. I wish I had a car of my own.

My mom hears me going through her purse. "What are you doing?" she asks.

"Getting the keys. It's my day to drive," I say, trying to get out of the room fast.

Mom is struggling to put on her robe. She says that I can't take the car today.

"You don't need the car!" I shout.

"Yes, I do—and you're not taking it!" she yells.

"You just want it to get more booze," I'm yelling as I head fast down the stairs.

Things happen so quick that I don't have time to think.

Mom might not have caught up with me if I hadn't stopped to get my books off the dining room table.

Mom has long nails. She can be very dangerous. She scratches and kicks. I try to get away, out through the kitchen. She's right behind me in the garage. The car is in the driveway. I hope it's not locked. Then I can make it inside and lock her out.

The car is locked.

It's hard to believe how strong a drunk can be. She grabs my hair. I've always been weaker than she is in a fight. She fights dirty—biting and kicking. This time I'm not letting her wreck my day or my carpool. I said I'd drive today and I will!

I dig my nails into her neck until she lets go of my hair. She grabs my hair again. I hit her with my fist, hard. Dad is coming out of the garage. He's yelling at us to stop.

I hit her harder this time. Her head flies back and her face twists toward the car roof. I can hear the sound of her head hitting the car. She turns around. There's blood all over her face. I can't believe how much blood is pouring out. It's starting to drip on the driveway. Maybe she'll die.

"I didn't mean to hit her that hard," I'm whining.

"Just get in the car and go to school. I'll take her to the hospital," Dad shouts as he leads Mom toward the garage.

"Is she going to be all right?" I ask.

"Just get going," says Dad.

* * *

I never mention what happened to my carpool friends on the way to school. How could they understand? I'm lucky we're not late for school.

I don't think I'm a mean person. I didn't want to hurt her that bad.

Last year there was a girl at my school named Marie. Her father killed himself. One morning, after Marie went to school, Marie's mom was doing the breakfast dishes. Her dad went into the garage and shot himself. Marie was at school when someone came in and told her that her dad was dead. I felt sorry for her.

I wonder if Mom will die today. Maybe someone will come to school and tell me she died. She could bleed to death.

Being an alcoholic is like committing suicide. It's slow, though. Mom should just get it over with. I wish she was brave enough to shoot herself. She's dying anyway.

Maybe if Mom was gone, Dad would stop drinking. He says he only drinks because it's the only way he can stand to live with Mom. I'm hoping every day that they'll get a divorce.

I don't want to be the one that kills her. I think about doing it. A couple of years ago, I took two loaded pistols that Dad keeps in his nightstand. I took off the safeties and gave one to my brother. Our parents were out. My plan was to shoot them when they came through the door. I don't think anyone would've blamed Gordie and me. We were going to say we thought they were robbers. We got tired of waiting. Finally, we put the guns back and made grilled cheese sandwiches.

I've had other plans to kill my mother. One is, I can push her down the stairs. Drunks fall all the time. The other plan is to put a bunch of the pills she takes all the time in her drink. You just empty the capsules and stir up the powder. It will look like an overdose; movie stars overdose all the time. The only thing that stops me is—if they did an autopsy, would they wonder where the capsules were, if they aren't in her stomach? I don't know. If I kill her, I might feel bad for the rest of my life—even if I get away with it!

It's funny how I feel today after hitting her head and cutting it open. I don't feel anything at all. I'm not even scared. I haven't cried in over a year. I'm proud of that. It shows I'm growing up.

Once Mom told me I was like a badger. If I get cornered, I can be real mean. Maybe I'm a cruel person without any feelings.

* * *

There is one guy I talk to, a little. Scott Day is in my art class. His mom is an alcoholic, too. We joke about how the drinking gets worse when there's a full moon. In fact, we think it's the moon's madness that makes our parents drink. It's nice to know someone has the same problems I do. Too bad I have drama class instead of art today. Scott would find a way to make this morning into a joke. He's the youngest in his family and one of the funniest people I ever met.

After school, Dad says the cuts on Mom's forehead from the car accident broke open when she hit the car. Her cuts aren't healing very well. I wonder if that's because she's got all that alcohol in her all the time.

CHAPTER 12

October 14, 1963

Im going crazy.

I didn't know I was going to pick this Saturday to go mad. I've been thinking about it, but I hadn't picked the day.

I have a book that describes what it's like to go crazy. It talks about what this guy felt like when he was insane. The book says, "It was like a gray, hissing fog, no noise, no one to bother him."

I've looked in medical books to see which mental illness is best. I decide it's <u>Catatonia.</u> All I have to do is not move. A catatonic stays in the same position all day long, never moving. If you put his arm in the air, it just says there. It sounds like being a piece of putty.

What makes me pick today is that this morning Dad tells me to clean the kitchen and rake the yard. I want to go uptown with Susan.

"You're not going anywhere, young lady, until you finish your chores," says Dad.

"It's not fair. Gordie never has to do anything. Besides, I

shouldn't have to do all the work just because Mom's too drunk to be a mother!" I yell at him.

"You'll do what I say, or you won't go out for the rest of the weekend!" yells Dad.

"Try and make me! I don't care what you think!" I scream.

"Don't you dare get hysterical with me. Start working!" Dad grabs me under my chin.

He always pinches the skin under my chin when he's mad at me. I hate it.

I break away from him.

"I'm going crazy in this house. I'm going crazy and there's nothing you can do to stop me!" I'm screaming as I run upstairs and lock myself in my bathroom.

"It'll be nice to be crazy!" I yell from behind the door.

Dad is cursing at me and shaking the door.

"I'm going to kill you when I get a hold of you!" he yells.

"I don't care! I'm gonna kill myself first!" I look for something to throw.

There's loads of stuff in the bathroom to hit the door with. At first, I feel guilty smashing bottles of perfume against it. By the fourth bottle, I'm getting the hang of it—except the smell is awful. I can hardly breathe!

This is fun! It's great to be the one smashing things for a change!

Once, when I was seven years old, my parents broke all the dishes and glasses in the kitchen. It was after I'd gone to bed. I can hear it happening. I'm sure someone will die. I take my teddy bear and go downstairs to stop them. I pick my biggest teddy bear because I think it will make me look smaller and more pitiful. Then I walk slowly through the broken glass. I have little tears in my eyes when I whisper, "Please, Mommy and Daddy, don't fight." They feel sorry for me and stop.

Now it's me breaking everything.

I'm pulling all the glass containers out of the cabinets and hurling them at the door. It's a great sound! Dad is still trying to get in. There are loads of things to break. I hit the door with a Listerine bottle. Now I'm into cleaning stuff—Pine Sol, Windex, Murphies Oil. Then medicine— cough syrup, eye wash. The bottles I can't break, I open and dump into one big mess: toilet bowl crystals, bubble bath, shampoo, conditioner, Comet. I wonder if the right mixture will explode. I'm down to squirting a can of shaving lotion on the mountain of goop.

Now I am insane. A quivering idiot. I'm sitting on the toilet seat—waiting for the "hissing fog" of madness to come for me.

I always knew I'd end up like this.

* * *

Dad gets into my bathroom by breaking the door.

He dumps me in bed. I will not answer him or talk at all. I stare straight ahead. I am a catatonic.

Mom is up now.

Gordie is trying to get me to eat potato chips.

They're talking about calling a doctor. It would be easy to give in and not be crazy, but I've made up my mind. I feel a little bad about my brother. He looks upset. He's never seen me freak out before. He's used to it with Dad and Mom, but not me. Dad looks worried, like he did the day we were all in the hospital on stretchers.

Boy, is time slow! Being bonkers is boring. I went insane at about ten o'clock this morning. It's only one thirty now. I'm doing well as a catatonic. It's not that hard. Except I'm getting a little hungry. I didn't eat breakfast. I wonder how catatonics eat. They must eat!

* * *

A doctor is here. It's the shrink my mom's been seeing. The one that gives her all the pills. I hear Dr. Greenburg coming upstairs with Dad. I wonder what he'll say. I wonder if he'll recognize that I'm catatonic. I hate him.

He checks me out. I don't move unless he moves me. I stare at the ceiling. He gives me a shot. I don't move. He talks to my dad like I'm not here.

Dr. Greenburg tells my dad I'm very disturbed. He hasn't figured out that I'm catatonic. I don't think he's a very good doctor. He's certainly not helping my mom.

"George, if she's not better by five o'clock, I believe the only thing to do is put her in a mental institution," says Dr. Greenburg.

"Which one?" asks Dad.

"Ludden State Mental Hospital is the closest one," says the doctor.

Dad doesn't say anything.

"George, I'd like to talk to you alone, downstairs," says Dr. Greenburg.

Then he looks at me. "Crissy, I don't think you'll like being in a mental institution. There are a lot of very sick people there. You won't like it."

I picture a place where people are yelling and cursing. It can't be much worse than it is at home.

＊ ＊ ＊

Part of me wants to stop being crazy. It's hard to stop once you start. This is probably how most people go insane. They start out pretending and then they can't stop.

I'm glad they went downstairs when they did. My nose is itching and it feels so good to scratch it!

＊ ＊ ＊

It's three forty-five. There's another problem. How do

catatonics go to the bathroom? I'm starting to have to go pretty bad.

Four o'clock. Susan is here. She's trying to joke me out of being crazy. It's getting hard not to laugh. She's talking about all the funny stuff that's ever happened to us, like the time we tried to scare Kathy Jenkins while she was babysitting. Kathy was sitting in a kitchen window at the Hiltons' when Susan and I started running toward the window. We forgot about the window wells around the basement window and we fell in them. Kathy says it was even scarier because she saw these faces coming toward her—then they suddenly disappeared. Susan and I scraped our legs falling in the wells, but it was worth it to see the look on Kathy's face.

Then Susan remembered the time Tammy Baldwin took her parents' car out and was worried they'd notice the mileage. We told her that if she drove the car backwards the mileage would go down. She drove around the block four times backwards before she noticed it didn't make any difference.

Then there was the time we gave Annie Harrison "near-beer" and told her she'd get drunk. She's doing summer-saults and acting drunk after just one. Susan is acting all this stuff out just like it happened. She's playing all the different parts.

I'm trying not to crack up—or wet my pants. I have to go bad!

Now she tells about the time we went skiing with the Camp and Trip Club in Junior High. Carry Sears and Jenny Phillips went with us. I ran into a tree at the top of the hill on a long run. I was hugging the tree, one ski on each side of it. The ski patrol came toward us to see if I'm hurt. I was afraid I'd fall backward down the hill if I let go of the tree. Carry and Jenny laughed so hard Carry wet her pants and left a big yellow spot in the snow.

Boy, do I have to go! I wish the medical books had explained about a catatonic going to the bathroom! I can't stand it anymore.

It's five thirty. I get up and go to the bathroom. Susan is happy. I go to the bathroom forever. Then we go downstairs and make popcorn with butter. She wants fudge. I'm not in the mood for it. My parents are feeling no pain. They've passed out.

* * *

No one, not even my dad, ever mentions my being crazy again.

CHAPTER 13

December 5, 1963

The last operation on my face was five weeks ago. Thanksgiving is over. My forehead looks better than I ever dreamed it could. I still wear bangs to cover the scars. Some people say I look cuter with my hair cut like this.

I meet a guy I like over the Thanksgiving weekend. His name is Tim Larsen. He's six feet two inches tall and has green eyes with long lashes. He goes to the University of Wisconsin. His parents only let him come home one weekend a month, so we write each other every day. His parents want him to get good grades. He only lives a few miles from my house. We never met before because he went to Culver Military for high school.

He got kicked out of there because he got caught with four cases of beer. He was so close to graduation they let him get his diploma. We haven't said we love each other yet. I sign my letters, "Love ya, Crissy." I think he's the guy I'm going to marry. We plan to spend every day with each other over Christmas vacation.

Today I find out in art class that the project I did with Scott Day won First Place. It goes in the main showcase during the Art Fair. Every year, the school has this art contest. All the winners' projects go on display in the lobby during December. Then they go to the First National Bank uptown for the month of January.

Scott and I never expect our project will win. It starts out as a joke between us. We want to sculpt a drunken family out of paper maché. We make the whole family look like clowns. We make clothes out of old ties. What probably wins it for us is the strange twisted positions of the people. We made everyone either being hurt or ignored. Everyone thinks it's the funniest sculpture they've ever seen.

Scott tells me he likes me after I tell him about Tim. I didn't know he liked me as a girlfriend because he's always joking around. It's too bad he didn't tell me before I meet Tim. I feel kinda bad about it. I like Scott—and, even though I tell him more about my parents than anyone else, he's always so funny that I never think of him without laughing. Those are the two good things that happen: meeting Tim, and winning the art contest.

Another thing happens that's terrible. A girl in my tenth grade class is stabbed to death by a senior boy. I didn't know either one of them. He stabbed her seven times with a knife as she was walking to school. It's awful to admit that something like that can make me feel better about my life . . . but it does.

When I first hear about it in biology class, I'm sad for the girl. I'm glad it wasn't me. It happened just a block from school. No one knows why he did it.

The guy was in Mr. Baird's English class. Mr. Baird is my drama teacher. He's telling us about it because he has to be out of school for a week to go to the kid's trial.

Mr. Baird says he volunteered to testify. This guy has been writing papers in English class about what he thought it would feel like to stick a knife into a living person. He wrote about it all the time. He wrote that it must be hard to cut into someone and kill him without hitting bones.

I ask Mr. Baird why he didn't report what the kid was writing to the police. Mr. Baird says he didn't take it seriously. He says lots of kids write things like that to shock the teacher.

I keep remembering all the time it took me to make up my life at home for my English Journal last year. I spent all that time making up what we ate for dinner and how wonderful we treated each other. Now, I think I could've written all the awful stuff that happened and no one would've believed it anyway. I could have written about wanting to kill my parents. I was afraid I'd be locked up for my thoughts!

The newspapers make a big deal about how such a tragic crime can take place in this nice, wealthy community. One article talks about how the kids living here have it made. That reporter should live at my house for a week! Actually, one night at my house could change his mind about how it is in Farfield Hills, Illinois!

* * *

It's as bad as ever at home. Mom is trying to sleep with me.

I end up sleeping in the spare room. I don't know why <u>she</u> doesn't go to the spare room. She's trying to tell me about her sex life with Dad. She says he doesn't like the dog in the room when they do it—and he likes to do sickening things. Parents should never talk about their sex life with their kids. It's disgusting!

Both my parents have a sex problem. I'm always having to tell my mother to put clothes on around my brother. I think she's trying to turn him on. She's using a douche bag one day and doesn't close the bathroom door. Gordie sees her. So do I.

Dad is just as bad. He stands in front of open windows and doors with nothing but his boxer shorts on. All the neighbors can see him. I tell him he can be arrested for indecent exposure. He yells at me that it's his own house and he'll do what he wants.

I worry about my little brother getting exposed to so much sex at his age.

Dad has <u>PLAYBOY</u> and other dirty magazines in a drawer in their bathroom. A couple of times, my girlfriends and I sneak them out. We sit around staring at the pictures and smoking cigarettes 'til we get dizzy. Dad also has some really gross pictures. Women doing all sorts of things with men and animals. How can anyone be so vulgar? I wonder what kind of person takes these pictures.

I know my brother looks at the pictures too.

Once, we find a movie of a woman and three guys. We run it on the projector in our entertainment room. Gordie and I watch it. Gordie's laughing the whole time. It's so sick! I have to admit, this one part does kinda turn me on. The rest is hard to watch. I wonder if all adults like pornography.

I can't believe my parents watch it.

When I go all the way I want it to be beautiful. I'll probably go all the way with Tim. Maybe at Christmas vacation.

Susan and I are talking to Vicki Randolph, who graduated last year. She says it's okay to go all the way if you're really in love. Before I do, I think I'll get on the pill. Only, I'm afraid to go to a doctor. Vicki says doing it with a rubber doesn't feel as good as doing it without one. She has a diaphragm because the pill made her gain weight. I don't want to gain weight either. I don't know what kind of birth control I'll use, yet.

I bet it's going to be scary the first time. Tim hasn't tried very hard yet. I'm glad I'm a virgin. I keep remembering the time with Bob Grayson when I was thirteen and he wouldn't do it. I was mad then. Now I'm glad.

The first time has to be in a bed, not in a car.

I wonder what my English teacher would have said last year if I'd written all this in my journal. She doesn't look like the type that has ever had sex.

Two weeks till Tim comes home for Christmas! He has four weeks off from college. I'm doing a lot better in school this year. At least I haven't been suspended or been in Mr. Burgess' office for fighting.

CHAPTER 14

February 22, 1964

Christmas sure didn't turn out the way I wanted it. Tim's parents only let him come home for the week between Christmas and New Year's. His grades are bad. If he doesn't get them up he'll be kicked out of college. So his parents make him get extra tutoring.

Christmas day is a disaster. I kind of expected it. Dad and my grandfather get into a fight about drinking. Grandpa says Mom and Dad shouldn't drink at all. He threatens to fire Dad. My grandfather owns the construction business where Dad is Vice-President. I wish Grandpa would fire Dad. I've been reading that sometimes when alcoholics lose their jobs, they stop drinking. Grandpa could hire him back again later on. My grandma says she and Grandpa don't want to meddle in my parents' business. I wish somebody wanted to.

Tim and I end up having Christmas dinner at the Big Boy. We take my little brother with us.

The rest of vacation, Tim and I take off every day in his car. We stop at the deli and get "monster sandwiches." I get a Coke. Tim always has beer. We park on this back road near a frozen pond. It isn't that cold parking in winter. We neck so much the car windows get steamed up. We almost go all the way a couple of times, but we don't because we don't have any birth control yet.

On New Year's Eve, Tim and I go to a party at Ron Wilson's house. His parents are gone. Someone brings grass and grain alcohol. I try the pot. I don't feel any different than I normally feel. Everyone says that I probably felt it but couldn't tell. I don't think it's any big deal.

The grain alcohol is very strong. I touch it to my lips and it burns all the way back on my tongue. I can't swallow it. That's good, because Tim gets sick from drinking so much. He pukes in the bathroom for half the night. I have to drive his car to my house. Tim falls asleep in our driveway. I'm afraid he'll freeze to death, but I leave him in the back seat. He says he woke up in the middle of the night and drove home okay.

Susan and I aren't getting along so hot. I think she's jealous of my going with Tim. She doesn't have a boyfriend. She says all I do is talk about Tim anymore.

Dad hates Tim. He calls him a bum. The feeling is mutual; Tim hates Dad too.

Dad asks me if we're having sex. I tell him it's none of his business. He slaps me in the face. I tell him to go ahead and hit me all he wants. He can't hurt me.

My parents have no right telling me how to live when they live the way they do.

* * *

During January, Tim and I write each other every day. He only comes home once. He says he's trying to get better grades. He hates college. When he doesn't come home on weekends, he calls me Saturday nights. We talk all night. Sometimes we fall asleep talking on the phone. Then, the phone is right there when we wake up in the morning. It's like spending the night together. Tim says it costs about eight dollars; that's about what a nice date costs anyway. I can't wait until we get married. Then we can wake up together every morning for the rest of our lives.

* * *

This is the last Saturday night in February. February is the most depressing month there is. Tim's coming home next weekend. I'm in my room waiting for his call. Dad walks into my room without knocking.

"Crissy, I'm going out. You stay here. Don't answer the door or anything," he says, looking mad and upset.

"What's the matter?" I ask.

"I don't know yet, but I'm sure as hell going to find out," says Dad as he leaves my room.

"Where's Mom?" I ask, thinking I haven't seen her all day.

"That's what I'm going to find out." Dad looks like he's going to explode.

I don't think I've ever seen Dad acting quite so angry. I follow him into his room. He takes one of his pistols out of the nightstand drawer and puts a clip in it.

"Dad, please tell me what's going on!" I'm scared now.

"I'll take care of it myself. After tonight I don't think there'll be any more problems," says Dad, as he shoves the gun in his belt.

"Please, Dad. Don't go out with a gun when you're mad," I beg him.

Dad pushes me aside as he heads downstairs.

"Dad, are you going to kill Mom?" I yell at him.

"I'm not going to kill her. I'll make her sorry she was ever alive!" he shouts.

"Dad, what's happened? Please! I have a right to know! She's my mother!" I yell as he puts on his coat and starts out of the garage.

"This is an adult matter. It doesn't concern you!" Dad yells back.

"BULLSHIT!" I scream.

He can't hear me. The electric garage door is going up. He's starting the car.

I don't know what to do. I feel like I should call someone. Grandpa? The police? Gordie is watching TV. I try calling Tim. The line is busy. It's eight o'clock already and he should have called me by now.

Eight thirty and Tim's line is still busy. I call the operator. I tell her it's an emergency. She has someone check the line.

It's out of order. She'll report it to repair. By the time it's fixed both of my parents will be dead.

Nine thirty. I call Susan. No one is home. The longer I wait for my parents to come back, the more I worry.

It's eleven o'clock. Tim's line is still out of order. I tell Gordie to go to bed. He says, "No."

Eleven twenty. Dad's car is coming up the driveway. Oh God, there's a police car behind him. My grandfather's car is behind the police car. I open the front door. Dad looks like he's been beaten up. His lip is swollen. His clothes are torn and his hands are bandaged.

Two policemen are holding Mom up between them. Her whole face is swollen up. Her eyes are black. There must have been a car accident, I think. I'm relieved. At least it wasn't a shooting! They wouldn't let Dad come home if he'd killed someone. My grandfather comes in last. He looks okay physically, but he's very upset. He has his pajama top on under his coat.

Dad tells Gordie and me to go to bed.

"I don't want to," I say. I want to know what happened.

"Take your brother and go to bed," says my grandfather. He looks at me in a way that I know we'd better go.

* * *

From my room, I can't overhear anything that's going on downstairs.

I sneak halfway down the stairs and can hear only a little of what they are saying. This is as close as I dare get. From here I can still get back to my room if someone's coming.

They're talking about putting Mom to bed. One of the cops asks if it will be safe. My grandfather says it will.

What else are they saying? Something about pressing charges...going to jail...a fine. Someone else is in the hospital. I can't hear who it is.

Dad is telling them everything is under control.

I wish I knew what happened. Gordie is nudging me and whispering, "What are they saying?"

They are talking too quietly to hear much. I hear Grandpa say something about, "...for the children's sake."

I scoot back to my room when I hear the voices coming closer. Gordie runs for his room. The cops are leaving. I can see them from my window. I don't want them to leave. I feel safe with them here. It's probably better if I stay in my room. Once when I was six or seven, Dad fired his gun in the house a couple of times. It was late at night. At first I thought I dreamed it, except I found bullet holes in my parents' room the next day. They moved the bureau in front of them. Then one day the bullet holes were gone. They just disappeared like it never happened.

I am tired. I pull the sheet up over my head. This whole family could disappear and it won't make any difference if I stay awake.

CHAPTER 15

February 23, 1964

Mom's been asleep all day. My grandfather is still here when I get up. I think he went home for a while because he has a shirt on instead of his pajama top. The phone has been ringing all morning. Dad and Grandpa are in the family room with the door shut. I try walking in and they tell me to leave.

One time when I answer the phone, a man says he's a reporter with the Farfield Hills Gazette. He wants to talk to Dad, but Dad won't talk to him. Tim calls. He says all the phones were out in Madison, Wisconsin last night. I tell him that something is going on and when I find out what it is I'll call him back.

It takes all day to get an idea what happened last night. Gordie and I take turns listening at the family room door and on the phone extension. Gordie hears something first.

"Mom was screwing our dentist and Dad caught them," he says, smiling because he figures out what happened first.

From what I hear, Mom was in the dentist's office with Dr. Roberts and Dad caught them. He smashed the plate glass window—I know how hard it is to smash a window! There was a big fight and Dr. Roberts is in the hospital.

I can't believe Mom is having an affair with the dentist. First of all, he's ugly. Second, why would anyone want to make love to a drunk like Mom? The other thing that bothers me is, if this is true, does this mean all my cavities are fake? Maybe Dr. Roberts said I had so many cavities just so he can see Mom. I have more fillings than anyone else I know. So does Gordie. We do eat tons of sweets though.

I wonder if my Dad will go to jail for beating up Dr. Roberts. I wonder how Dr. Roberts' wife feels. I wonder how his kids feel! He's got kids in college. This is terrible. I'm going to be so ashamed if anyone in school hears about this. I'm not going to tell Tim. I can't.

* * *

Susan listens to the whole thing. Then she says she's gotta go study. I wish I hadn't told her. I can tell she's embarrassed.

CHAPTER 16

February 27, 1964

I'd give anything not to have to go to school this morning.

The story is all over the place. A bunch of guys walk past me between first and second period. One of them yells, "Hey, I hear your mom's getting drilled in the dentist's chair!"

I pretend like I don't hear them. By the time I get to art class, I know everyone is talking about it. I ask Scott Day to tell me what he's heard. He treats it like a joke, like he does everything. He says the kids are saying my dad pulled a parking sign out of the ground, one that was cemented into the sidewalk. Then he smashed the window to get inside the dentist's office. Everyone says Dad beat up Mom and the dentist. When the cops got there, he was holding a gun on both of them. Someone told Scott that Mom and Dr. Roberts were stark naked. No one knows who called the cops.

It's a good thing the cops got there when they did. Dad was going to kill both of them.

I'm trying to walk around and pretend like nothing is

wrong. I can't look anyone in the eyes. I'm watching my feet as I walk down the hall. I'm okay until I'm passing the principal's office. Mr. Burgess sees me. I walk faster, but I can tell he's going to talk to me. He puts his hand on my shoulder and asks if I'm okay.

I start to cry. After that I can't stop. I just keep on bawling. It's like I have a lot of crying stored up inside me. He puts his arm around me and pulls me into his office, calling for the nurse. She rubs my hand. They want me to talk, but I can hardly catch my breath. I just keep crying. My nose runs—I look awful. It's terrible.

Finally Mr. Burgess decides to drive me home. I cry all the way; I cry when I get inside; I cry lying on my bed; I cry until I fall asleep.

The next day I don't even wake up until ten thirty. I have to put ice on my eyes because they're just about swollen shut from all that crying.

March 3, 1964

I haven't been back to school since. I told Tim not to come home last weekend because I'm sick. I don't want to tell him. Mr. Burgess calls this morning to see how I am. He wants to know when I'm coming back to school. I tell him I'm very sick with the flu. I cough to prove it. I don't think my parents have even noticed how long I'm staying home.

I may not be lying about being sick. I <u>do</u> feel terrible. I have no energy at all. I sleep almost all day and all night.

The good thing is that I've lost 12 pounds. I'm not hungry at all.

The reason I'm worried I might really be sick is that there are all these lumps in my neck. They're huge. The ones behind my ears are the size of walnuts. There are more lumps in my armpits and at the top of my legs. I took my temperature this morning. It's ninety nine point seven. That's not very high. But the lumps are tender and sore.

From looking in the medical books, I know what the lumps are. They're lymph nodes. The book says there are lots of them in the neck, armpit, and the groin. When they get swollen it means the person is very sick. I've found three illnesses this can be. It's either Hodgkin's disease, leukemia, or mononucleosis. I hope it's mono. They call that the "kissing disease." People must spread it by kissing. The other two diseases are killers. They're cancer. I haven't told my parents. They don't care.

I find a doctor in the yellow pages. I make an appointment and go to see him. I don't want to go to our family doctor. I don't trust anyone after this thing with my mom and our dentist.

I use a fake name. I also lie about my age. I say I'm eighteen and living alone.

Tim is home this weekend. I feel too rotten to do much of anything. He feels the lumps. He wants me to go to his family's doctor. The doctor I found in the yellow pages took a blood test. He says it will be ready on Monday. He wants to call me to tell me the results. I tell him I don't have a phone so I'll have to call him. I don't think he believes me about being eighteen and living alone. He wants to know where I work. I say I'm living on some money I saved up.

Tim and I spend most of the weekend in my room watching TV. I don't think we should kiss or anything because Tim might get sick too. Tim says he doesn't care. I hope I don't have leukemia. I'd hate to die now that I'm in love!

* * *

Monday afternoon I call the doctor's office. The nurse says the doctor wants to see me. I tell her I can't get there because my car is being repaired.

The doctor gets on the phone and says the test is negative for mono. He wants me to come in so he can run some more tests. He says it's very important for me to go back. I tell him I'll make an appointment when my car is fixed. I hang up fast. I don't plan to go back.

I know now I have either Hodgkin's disease or leukemia. I've been reading what they do to you. They use chemotherapy and X-rays. Once they start doing that, all your hair falls out and you're sick to your stomach all the time. I don't want to die like that.

I feel lousy. I don't want to live at all.

March 12, 1964

I go back to school. I fall asleep in most of my classes.

Then I come home and go right to bed. I don't wake up again until it's time to go to school. I have to set my alarm twice. Once, for ten o'clock at night. Then I set it again for seven o'clock in the morning. When you go to sleep at three thirty in the afternoon, if you set the alarm for seven if goes off at seven in the evening.

I've lost 18 pounds all together now. That's one good thing about dying!

I haven't figured who to give all my stuff to when I die. I want to leave some things to my brother, like my TV and desk. There are some things, though, only a girl could want. Susan hardly ever calls me anymore. I'm trying to think of something special to leave Tim. He says he's worried about me. We had a fight on the phone last night. He's been calling and waking me up almost every night. He wants me to go to another doctor.

It's been almost four weeks since I got sick. Tim's been home three times. He bought a car that his parents don't know about. They also don't know he's coming home all the time. He stays at Ron Wilson's house. He wants to quit school. He asked me to marry him. He says he can work at one of the factories.

Before I die I want to make love. Tim and I have decided to rent a hotel room this weekend and do it. It won't matter if I get pregnant because I won't live that long anyway.

CHAPTER 17

March 22, 1964

This is the day Tim and I are going to make love. We figure a Friday night is good. Then we can stay all day Saturday and Saturday night too, if we like it. I'm not saying a word to my parents. They may not notice I'm gone. I'm laying in bed daydreaming about the weekend.

I decide not to go to school today. I want to save all my energy for the weekend. I must be getting near dying soon. It takes every bit of strength I have just to do normal junk like brush my teeth.

It's funny. I'm not scared of going all the way like I used to be. Dying does that to you.

Finally at noon I get up to go to the bathroom.

Oh, my God! My face! My stomach! I'm covered with red marks everywhere! I don't remember reading about anything like this happening in the medical books. I'm much closer to dying than I thought!

This ruins everything. I look terrible! Tim will never want to even kiss me now. I pictured myself dying skinny and beautiful, not all red and blotchy! It doesn't itch or anything so it can't be measles or chickenpox. I think I've had them anyway.

Back to the medical books. I've got to find a disease with swollen lymph nodes and a red rash.

I'm still going through the medical books when Tim gets here at four o'clock.

"Crissy, you're going to the doctor's right now!" Tim says as soon as he sees me. He doesn't believe I'm dying.

As soon as Dad comes home, Tim tells him to look at me. Dad gets all upset and calls Dr. Cunningham. He's our regular doctor.

Dr. Cunningham is coming to the house. He only lives a few blocks away. Dad says he's stopping here on his way home.

To tell the truth, I'm glad he's coming. I don't want to admit it, but I've been a little worried.

Dr. Cunningham takes my temperature and checks out all the swollen lumps.

"Crissy, your lymph nodes are quite swollen. You have one of the worst cases of mononucleosis I've ever seen," he says.

I decide to tell him everything.

"Dr. Cunningham, I don't have mono. I went to this doctor and he took a test for mono. It was negative." I start to tell him about Hodgkin's disease or leukemia when he interrupts me.

"Crissy, I don't know who you saw or what kind of test he took. I don't know if a mistake was made on the test," he says. "What I <u>do</u> know is that you have mono. You're going to be just fine with some vitamins and lots of rest."

Dr. Cunningham is just great. He explains how teenagers who live under a lot of stress sometimes get mono when their bodies can't take it anymore. He says he knows both of my parents are alcoholics.

"This is not easy for you, Crissy, living like this, but you <u>can</u> make a nice life for yourself. You will have to realize that you need to take care of yourself. Your parents are too sick to take care of you," he says. I know he's telling me the truth.

I ask him why he can't make my parents stop drinking.

Dr. Cunningham says that alcoholics can't get better until they really want to. That has to come from inside of them. He can't make them do it. He says it isn't my fault they're alcoholic.

I can't believe he knows that I think it's my fault. He's saying things like he can read my mind.

"Crissy, many alcoholics <u>do</u> get better. But your mom's pretty far gone," he says.

"Do you mean she's gonna die?" I ask.

"She could. And it's not a very pleasant way to die," he answers.

Then, like he's reading my mind again, he says that he doesn't know how much longer she can go on like this.

He knows how terrible it is living here!

He says he thinks Tim is a very nice young man. Then, out of the blue, he asks, "Are you and Tim having intercourse?"

I can feel my face burning. I say, "No."

"Are you going to?" he asks.

He is being so nice I don't want to lie. I nod my head yes.

"Crissy, I want you to promise me you won't do anything until you get well. That's going to be quite a few weeks. I want you healthy first." He pauses. "I don't think you should have intercourse until you're older. I'm not telling you not to, because that's your choice. But I'm strongly suggesting that you wait. Okay?"

"Okay, I promise," and I mean it, right now.

"I'm going to be seeing you every week until you're healthy again. Just remember that I'll be available to talk about birth control when you're ready."

"Can I have the pill?"

"I don't know. That may be best. We'll talk about it later."

"All right," is all I can say.

"Right now, you'll have to roll over. I'm giving you two shots. One will help you rest. The other is a vitamin shot. I'm giving your dad a prescription for you to take too. Follow the directions exactly."

"Are you sure I don't have leukemia or Hodgkin's disease?" I ask.

He smiles at me. "I'm positive, Crissy. I'm going to take a blood test anyway, although I really don't have to. I know what you have is mono."

One of the shots stings.

"Crissy, I'm going to tell your dad the same things I'm telling you. You can't have any disturbances. You need absolute bed rest and quiet. Someone will have to bring you your meals so you can stay in bed. Completely in bed! The only time I want you getting up is to go to the bathroom," he says as he starts to leave my room.

"If you don't stay quiet you'll be sick a lot longer. Understand?"

"Can I take a shower? I feel icky if I don't take a shower every day," I ask.

"Yes, you can take a shower, but that's it. I want you reading or watching TV, in bed."

"When can I go back to school?" I ask him. I don't care about going back. I just want to know how long I can stay home.

"I don't know. We'll see. You'll be out of school for a few

weeks at least. Someone will have to call the school. I'll take care of that with your dad." Dr. Cunningham pats me on the head. He stops at the door and says, "Stop reading those medical books. Let me be the doctor."

CHAPTER 18

April 4, 1964

It's not bad being sick, now that I know I don't have to think about dying anymore. Dr. Cunningham comes by every Tuesday evening around dinnertime. He says I'm doing fine. All I do is stay in bed all day. The school is sending home a bunch of work. They arrange it so I can drop out of Spanish and still pass into my senior year. I've been home three weeks already. It's almost the end of April.

One of the best things about being home is that Dad hired Eloise to come every day. She's so nice to me. She fixes all my food. I don't want to eat too much. I don't want to gain back the weight I lost. Kids from school have been stopping by. They say I look great. I feel kinda pretty.

Dad has been bringing home this delicious hard salami. It's my favorite thing to eat on white bread with mustard. I usually don't eat the dinner Eloise leaves. I'd rather have salami and pistachio nuts. I'd never tell Eloise that I don't eat her dinner. That would hurt her feelings.

Whatever Dr. Cunningham told my parents, it's working. I haven't heard a fight the whole time I've been sick. I don't know what Mom does all day. That's a good part about living in a big house.

A big chair was moved into my room so Tim can sit with me when he's home on weekends.

Aunt Martha buys me two new nightgowns and some books to read. Tonight I start reading <u>Man Child In The Promised Land</u> by Claude Brown.

This is the first time I can remember having a peaceful life.

It's hard to describe, but the house smells better since I've been sick.

The house smells like the turkey Eloise is cooking.

When Eloise changes my sheets, she rubs my back. Sometimes I wonder how she feels about taking care of us. I try to get her to talk about her life, but she won't say much. I want to ask her what it's like to have breast cancer, but I'm afraid to mention it. It might make her feel bad. Besides, we're not allowed to talk about bad things in my house.

* * *

I can hear the garage door opening. Dad must be home. He's been bringing home all these great treats to eat, like boxes of Dunkin' Donuts and bags of M&M's.

Dad comes into my room with a pint of ice cream. It's half Chocolate and half French Vanilla—my favorite. Dad shouldn't eat any of the stuff; he weighs almost 300 pounds.

"Crissy, there's something I want to discuss with you," he says as he hands me the ice cream.

I take it and say, "Go ahead, Dad."

He sits in the easy chair and says, "Your mother and I are getting a divorce."

The minute he says it, the thought of eating the ice cream makes me sick. He's so calm. He's always been threatening to divorce Mom. He's yelled "I'll divorce you!" at her whenever they're fighting for as long as I can remember. This time he isn't even acting mad.

I don't know what to do with the ice cream.

"Crissy, did you hear me? Your mother and I are getting a divorce."

"What does this mean?" I ask.

"It means that you and your brother are going to have to decide who you want to live with. I saw the lawyer today. You and your brother are both old enough to help decide who you want to live with," he says.

Dad looks smaller than I've ever seen him look. His fat looks like someone took the inside out of a toasted marshmallow.

"Where will we live?" I ask.

"If the Judge gives me custody, we'll go on living right here," he says.

"What will happen to Mom?"

"I'll take care of her. I'll help her find a place to live," he says.

"What does Mom have to say about this?" I ask.

"Your mother has been gone for four days now," Dad says.

Well, it's true I don't remember seeing her around. Still, it's a shock.

"You mean she moved out already?" I ask.

"Yes," says Dad. I can't tell if he's breathing.

"Is she with the dentist?" I ask, thinking they might have run away together.

"No, she's with some other guy she met at one of those Alcoholics Anonymous meetings," he answers. Dad is being honest.

I didn't know she was going to A.A. meetings.

"Did she stop drinking?" I ask.

"No, they're both drinking," he answers.

"I can't believe it! She ran away with another alcoholic?"

"Crissy, I don't want to talk about it, okay? I need to know who you want to live with," he says quietly.

"Gordie and I will live with you," I say, knowing my brother will do whatever I do.

"Good. I hope you won't change your mind. This could get rough," says Dad.

He's getting up to leave. "Crissy, I want you to know I hoped this would never happen. There has never been a divorce in my family," he says as he leaves, looking like an old dough boy.

I let the ice cream melt on my nightstand.

A little part of me is happy. I wanted this to happen. I never thought it would be like this. Dad is talking so nice. I never thought they'd actually get divorced.

I know I'll stay with Dad. He's not as drunk as Mom all the time. I don't know how Mom would take care of Gordie and me.

I feel guilty. One of the reasons I'm staying with Dad is because he has all the money. I know it's selfish. Mom could probably use me to take care of her.

If I was a better person, I'd go with Mom.

Dad was mean to Mom many times. That could be why she drinks. This may have happened because of the affair Mom had with the dentist. It's sickening that a mother would go to bed with another man. But there were all those times I watched her try to be affectionate with Dad. Once, she tried to sit on his lap and he pushed her on the floor. She was just trying to be nice.

I know Dad goes to bed with other women. When I was twelve, we were going to Florida for vacation. The night before we left, there was a big fight. I didn't know what happened at the time. I overheard things later. It seems Mom caught Dad at my grandparents' house with two women. They were in my grandmother's bedroom. Mom scratched Dad's eye so bad that he had to wear sunglasses the whole time we were in Florida and for two weeks afterwards.

Somehow it doesn't seem so bad for a man to do it.

* * *

Gordie crawls into bed with me to watch TV. He's upset. I try to get him to stop scratching his hands and feet; they're bleeding all over my clean sheets.

Dad is sitting in his green recliner drinking a bottle of vodka.

Nobody remembers to take Gigi out. She went to the bathroom on my parents' bed.

CHAPTER 19

April 9, 1964

Strange how it is: I lose one person, and at the same time I lose other people I don't even know are going.

Like when Grandma died. The day I found out, all I could think about was losing Grandma. She was the one who died. I didn't realize it at the time, but on the same day I lost my grandfather too. He was my mother's father. He called Mom and told her she'd killed her mother with all her problems. I never cried over him like I did Grandma. Just the same, it's like he died that day. I only saw him once afterwards.

The day after Grandma died, my other grandparents picked me and Gordie up at my aunt's house. They took us to the funeral parlor. My mom's sister, my aunt Cathy, was there. She was crying. Her eyes were all swollen. Still, she looked good. She had makeup on to cover her face. Her tears kept rolling to the end of her nose. She wiped them away with a handkerchief.

Then there was Mom. She was blubbering all over the place. She kept swaying from side to side. Her face was a mess. I didn't want to stand next to her.

I should have had an idea of what was happening.

Grandma was lying there in the coffin. She looked nice, but dead. Everyone kept saying how nice she looked. Grandma looked better dead than Mom looked alive! Really!

I could tell Dad wasn't getting along with Grandpa because they stayed at opposite sides of the room.

On the way home, my other grandparents talked about how rotten Grandpa was. They said my dead grandmother was the one who had loved us kids. She did.

I tried calling Grandpa a couple of times. He was nice on the phone, but he never called me. At Christmas every year he sent Gordie and me twenty-five dollars each. They were always clean, new bills he glued together on cardboard like a pad of paper. To spend the money I pulled the bills off one at a time.

When Grandma died, it changed my whole life a lot more than just her never being here. I lost Grandpa, and the way I see it I lost my real mom too. I've never seen her sober since the funeral.

* * *

It's happening the same way with my parents getting divorced. Today Dad is staying home from work. Eloise is here as usual. I can hear them in the kitchen. Then I don't hear anything all morning. I'm reading My Cousin Rachel. Eloise brings me one of my salami sandwiches at noon. She says I'm gonna turn into a salami if it's all I eat.

The quiet finally gets to me. I go downstairs to see what's going on. The first floor is empty. I go through all the rooms. I start down the basement stairs looking for Eloise and Dad.

"Oh, Mr. Mahr, I never knew." That's Eloise talking.

"It's hard to believe." That's Dad.

I creep down the stairs quietly, only looking at one stair at a time. That's why it's such a shock when I get to the sixth step from the bottom. The stairs are covered with empty Scotch bottles!

Eloise and Dad are still pulling empty bottles of Cutty Sark and Johnnie Walker Red out of the rafters in the fruit cellar.

Now I know why Mom spent all her time in the entertainment room. All those bottles! No wonder she was drunk all the time!

Eloise looks up at me as she starts to carry the bottles upstairs. "Honey, you goes on back to bed now. Nothin' to be done."

* * *

The next day Eloise brings me toast and Coke for breakfast. She's quit telling me about Coke not being good for me.

Instead of opening all the curtains in my room, she just opens one. Then she sits on the end of the chaise lounge.

"Crissy, I's been with you and you mama since you was born. I loves you and little Gordie. But I ain't gettin' younger."

"Oh, Eloise, you look great!" I say. It's true. She's lost almost half of herself in weight since her breast was taken off.

"Hush child—listen to me. You's almost a lady now." Eloise looks like she'll cry. "It's sad what's happening to you mama."

Eloise stops. She's holding her breath. So am I.

"I loves you mama. Youse don't know... you mama's a fine woman. Fine as they come. I knows her. I knows what's wrong with her. She scared, ... scared to death of people. Why, she be the most gentlest, kindest lady I's ever met." Eloise looks at her hands before she continues.

"Ain't many people in this whole world like her. Why, I's remember comin' into work and findin' she's walking all night with you. You's the most colicky baby!"

I want to tell Eloise that I loved my mom when I was little. But . . .

"Don't youse go saying anythin', Crissy. Y'hear me out. I promise you mama I stays and helps you and Gordie. I knows you dad calls me nigger. I knows you brother talks bad about colored folk. I stays 'cause of you mama. She ain't never has a mean bone in her body. You daddy and you mama just plain bad for each other." Eloise stops to see if I'm listening. I am.

"You's just like you mama. You's always doin' too much thinkin'...just like her. Ya got too many feelin's. I been seein' things. I been seein' everyone hurtin' in this house. It's over now. You mama's gone. You the lady. Youse gotta take care of things."

Eloise looks tired. I don't want to interrupt her.

"You knows I got the cancer. I ain't never got no better from it. My arm can't hardly lift nothin'. Takin' all those bottles down yesterday—set my arm a jumpin'." Eloise is rubbing her shoulder.

A sick feeling is starting in my stomach. I can't drink any more of my Coke.

"Honey, I be goin'. I ain't stong 'nough no more," says Eloise.

She's waiting for me to say something. I can't think of this house without Eloise.

"You can't!" I protest.

"Honey, the day you's back to school be my last day." Eloise says.

"Who'll take care of us?" I ask.

Gracious Lord! Girl, you be old 'nough to take care of youself," Eloise says.

"Eloise, I love you," I say. I don't usually say that to anyone.

"I knows that. You be fine without me."

"Where will you go, Eloise?" I don't want to know. This isn't right.

"Home to Mississippi where I's belong."

* * *

I lie in bed a long time after Eloise goes back downstairs, thinking about life without her. I didn't know that when Mom left, Eloise would go too.

Yesterday, I find out Mom and Dad are getting a divorce. Today Eloise is leaving. It isn't fair!

CHAPTER 20

April 21, 1964

Dr. Cunningham checks me out. He wants to know if I'm staying in bed resting. He says my glands are still very swollen. He doesn't understand why I'm not getting any better. He says it's taking much longer than he expected.

That's okay with me. The longer I'm sick, the longer Eloise stays with us. I'm hoping I can change her mind about leaving.

This morning, when Eloise is out doing the grocery shopping, I go down to the fruit cellar. It's supposed to be for storing food, but it's filled with boxes and trunks. Lots of old things are stored down there. Two old toy chests are filled with my dolls. I have so many dolls I never named them all. There are baby dolls, boy dolls and Madame Alexanders. Madame Alexanders are my favorites. I have most of the Little Women—Beth, Jo and Amy.

There are tons of clothes for all my dolls. Someday I'm going to wash and iron every one of them.

Today I'm looking for something else. An old trunk of my mother's.

I haven't felt sad about her being gone yet. It's not like we were getting along. We haven't been close these last four years. What I want to know is why. Why does she drink like that? Why is she an alcoholic? Why did Mom and Dad fight so much?

People say lots of things like, "The acorn doesn't fall very far from the tree," and "Like mother, like daughter." I'm afraid if I don't find out why it happened to Mom, it'll happen to me. I swear I'll never be like her. But, what if it's an inherited disease? One of the books I read on alcoholism says that it is. I don't see how it can be. It's awful to think I can end up like her.

There's a girl I can't stand in my homeroom. One morning she's talking real loud. She knows I'm listening. She knows about my mom and the dentist. She's talking to two guys, and she says, "... if you want to see how a girl is going to turn out, all you have to do is look at her mother." That hurts me. I know she wants to hurt me, so I act like I don't hear it. Her mother is in good shape and she's always working on the PTA or her picture is in the paper for some charity affair.

I find Mom's old trunk, but it's locked. I remember a bunch of keys on top of the armoire chest in my parents' dressing room.

* * *

There must be fifty keys on this ring. I'm worried that Eloise will get home before I find the right one. The seventh one does it. There are stacks of old letters, books, pictures and spiral pads filled with Mom's writing. There's no time to look at anything now. I pick a couple of letters from each stack, two spiral notebooks and a leather-bound datebook.

I move fast. I barely have time to push the trunk back under the stairs, put the keys back and hide the stuff under my bed before I hear Eloise calling, "Yoo-hoo, I's here."

* * *

It's taking days and days to read all the letters and things. I've made a lot of trips to the basement. I have to wait until everyone's gone to sneak down and get more. I feel guilty. I know it's wrong reading someone else's mail. It's strange. There's one stack of letters that Mom wrote and never mailed. They're to a man in California named John Wilcox. I've heard of him. She wrote some after my parents were married, some even after I was born. They're the only writing that makes much sense to me. The rest is poetry and long descriptions of places.

From what I can figure out, Mom was in love with this John Wilcox when she married Dad. I can't figure out when my parents were actually married. I always thought it was a couple of years before I was born, but now I'm not so sure.

Dad was in World War Two. I've heard the stories of how he got the Purple Heart. He volunteered to put out a chemical fire. The fumes damaged his lungs, and he was in a VA hospital for six months. Now his lungs are permanently damaged. He gets a check from the government every month.

If they were married before Dad went to war, then it's for

sure that Mom still had something going with this John Wilcox. There are letters from him to her, during the time Dad was in the war and in the VA hospital. He wanted her to come to California. He wanted to marry her. I don't understand why Mom wrote him all those letters and never mailed them. This John keeps asking why she won't write more often, so she must have mailed some of the letters she wrote.

* * *

This morning I find some writing that sort of explains things. It's a page in one of Mom's spiral notebooks. Almost all of her writing is about nature, love and junk. This one says that my grandmother Mahr (my dad's mom) had found divorce papers for my parents in my dad's laundry. It says that both my parents and their parents had a big meeting and it was decided they would stay married. They'd never lived together. Now I know what happened. That was written five months before I was born.

I was the cause of everything. If it hadn't been for me, my parents would've gotten divorced years ago. All the drinking and fighting would never have happened.

Is my dad really my dad? Maybe John Wilcox is my father? Mom obviously saw him while she was married to Dad. The only thing that stops me thinking that is that I look so much like my dad when he was young.

It must have been a terrible marriage from the beginning. A leather date book from the time I was two years old has this written in it: "The baby is the only person I live for. I am consumed by her, loving her. I know it's unhealthy to be this close to her. George works all the time, trying to be the successful young businessman working at his father's company. He never has time for Crissy or me . . ."

One of the last letters I read this morning is another of those unmailed letters to John Wilcox. Mom tells him how, when I was born, Dad just dropped her off at the hospital and went home. She wrote that Dad's mom, my grandma, had to make him go back to the hospital. He didn't want to bring me home because I was a girl.

All this happened because of me. I didn't ask to be born!

April 27, 1964

Dr. Cunningham says I can go back to school on Monday. It's been seven weeks since I've been out of the house.

Tim will be home this weekend. It'll be the first time we can go out. Tim's flunking out of college. His parents don't know that yet.

Dad has been very nice to me. He never bothers me. I think part of the reason he's being so nice is that a social worker is coming next week to talk to Gordie and me. The court is sending her. They do that to decide who gets custody. Maybe he's afraid we'll change our minds about living with him.

I have this hope that when the social worker gets here, she'll straighten things out. I've waited my entire life to tell someone what happens in this house—someone who knows what to do about it.

Dad sits in his green chair every night getting drunk. He's lonely without Mom to fight with anymore. I haven't seen or heard from Mom since she left. I wonder if I'll ever see her again.

* * *

Today is Eloise's last day. I still can't believe she's really going. I ask Dad if she can come and live with us. He says we can't afford to keep Eloise any longer. He yells about how much Mom's lawyers are trying to get. He says Mom took all the credit cards and charged a bunch of stuff to him.

I don't know how I'll say goodbye to Eloise.

Tim is coming over at noon. We're going to our favorite parking place, then to the movies.

Dad doesn't usually get home until five or six o'clock. That's why I'm surprised to see him before lunch.

"How come you're home?" I ask.

"I'm driving Eloise home. It's her last day and she has quite a few things to take with her," he answers.

"Eloise has her own car," I say, not understanding.

"She took the bus today. Her arm has been worse lately. I told her I'd take her," he says.

"Tim can help," I offer. "He'll be here in a little bit. We're going out."

"No, you're not!" Dad commands.

"Oh, yes, I am! Dr. Cunningham says I'm fine and I can do anything I want!" I yell.

"You're not going anywhere except to school on Monday. I won't hear another word. That's it!" his voice is louder.

"You can't make me do anything!" I'm getting nasty.

"Go to your room, young lady!" he shouts.

None of what happens next would have happened if it wasn't Eloise's last day and Dad hadn't come home early.

Tim is walking up to the back door when he hears us yelling. He walks right in without knocking. Dad tries to grab me under the chin. I run around the kitchen table. Tim orders Dad to leave me alone. That makes Dad super mad. He takes off after Tim. They're yelling and swearing at each other. Tim yells, "Run for the car!" and throws me his car keys. I miss the catch. By the time I pick them up and race out the door, Dad is trying to punch Tim. Tim is ducking.

Tim yells, "Get the car started, Crissy!"

It takes two tries to start it. Tim is running toward the car with Dad close behind. Tim jumps in the driver's side and pushes me out of the way.

"Lock the doors!" he shouts.

Just in time I lock my side as Dad grabs the handle.

When Dad realizes he can't get in, he starts kicking the car. We drive off with Dad cussing at us.

We go to our favorite parking place by the pond. The world has changed. I've been inside since the beginning of

March. Now all the leaves are out. It's beautiful. Tim and I talk all afternoon until dark. We decide to run away together. His aunt and uncle have a cabin in northern Michigan that no one uses until June. Tim doesn't care about going back to school. He's flunking out and he knows his parents will be furious.

The only problem is that we have only eleven dollars and the gas tank is less than a quarter full. We'll have to wait until tomorrow when the bank opens. Tim has a savings account with almost two hundred dollars in it. We have to find a place to hide, tonight. We can get jobs when we get up north. I know Dad will call the police. We can't stay here. This is a place where the cops know kids park. That's why we only come here during the day.

We're starved. We go to the Party Store and spend six dollars on food. that leaves five dollars for gas in the morning. Then we'll go to the bank. Tim says he has an idea where we'll hide tonight.

"Tell me, where?" I ask.

"You'll be surprised," Tim says, laughing.

I sure am surprised! He heads straight for the high school.

"Tim, this is one of the first places they'll look for us," I protest.

"Not where we're going."

Tim drives through the parking lot, over the curb, across the baseball field, over the archery range, and stops behind a clump of bushes near the cross-country track. He's right. No one will find us here!

We make love for the first time in the back seat. Tim doesn't want to do it. He's worried about birth control. I sort of force him to do it. We use withdrawal as birth control. He pulls out just before he comes.

It's okay, but it was over too quick.

* * *

We wait until seven o'clock to drive out. We want to be sure the gas station is open. I go to the restroom. When I come out, the cops are standing there.

Tim and I ride in the back seat of the police car to the police station. We were dumb to pick a gas station so close to the police station! The cops say they've been looking for us all night. What they really want to know is where we hid out. Tim gives me a look that I know means not to tell.

We sit in the station waiting for our parents. This is embarrassing. I've never met Tim's parents before.

Dad shows up first. His eyes are shooting daggers. I'm afraid he's going to kill me. I try telling the police I'm afraid of him. They say I'm under age. I yell at them that Dad's a drunk. Dad's face is as mean as I've ever seen it.

"You're never going to see my daughter again!" Dad tells Tim.

I stand up fast and yell over my shoulder, "You can't stop

us from seeing each other!" I run for the door. I run across the field. Tim is right behind me.

"Head for those trees!" Tim yells.

We never make it to the trees. One cop grabs me and the other one tackles Tim. They're fast.

I don't know why, but I get the feeling the cops think this whole thing is funny.

Tim's parents pull up to the station just as we're walking back in. His mom and dad look nice. They're dressed up. His mom has on a mink coat. His dad is wearing a suit and tie.

Tim's parents ask to talk to Tim alone. The police put them in a little room and shut the door. Mr. Larsen asks Dad if he'd mind waiting until they talk to their son before taking me home.

That's the first time I know for sure I won't be jailed for running away.

Dad and I glare at each other from across the room. A cop sits next to me. He's afraid I'll run for the door again.

After almost twenty minutes, Tim comes out with his parents.

Mr. Larsen says to my dad, "Mr. Mahr, may we talk with you a moment?"

"Call me George," says Dad, walking into the room with

them. He's acting nice in front of the Larsens. The door shuts.

Tim sits down next to me and holds my hand.

One of the policemen says, "You two kids sure have a lot of energy." He's smiling.

Tim leans over and whispers to me, "I won't let your dad hurt you."

When our parents finally come out, they're all smiles.

Mrs. Larsen says, "We need to talk to both of you, together."

Tim's dad interrupts. "I'll bet you're both hungry. We're going to our house for breakfast."

Mr. Larsen turns to the cop sitting next to me. "Officer, is it all right if we take the kids home now?"

"It's fine. I hope you get this matter straightened out."

It's decided that Tim and I can ride together with his dad. Mrs. Larsen is going to ride with my dad to show him the way.

I can't tell what Dad's thinking.

All I can think of is, I never got to say goodbye to Eloise. Yesterday was her last day. Now she's gone. It was the same with my mother.

* * *

Mrs. Larsen cooks breakfast. Mr. Larsen makes Bloody Marys.

Breakfast is a nervous time. The parents ask us all kinds of questions like, did we have any idea how much groceries and renting a place to live would cost. They're surprised that our answers are as good as they are. They ask if they need to worry about me getting pregnant. Tim and I both say, "No!" We act mad that they can even think of such a thing.

I'm relieved when it's all over. They make us promise to obey certain rules like when we can go out and what time we have to be home. Tim and I agree.

I sleep all day Saturday.

CHAPTER 22

October 23, 1964

First marking period of my Senior year is over. All my grades were D's, except for an A in art class.

I'm sitting in civics class staring at the light reflecting on my engagement ring. Sometimes it's blue or red fire. Tim surprised me with it on my birthday. I knew we were getting married, but I didn't expect a ring until Christmas. It's a one-carat emerald-cut diamond set in white gold. If I get it just right, I can see my eye shining back at me.

Our wedding is planned for the week after I graduate. I won't be eighteen then, but Dad will give his permission anyway. Tim and I think our parents are going along with all this because they hope we'll change our minds. I don't know what else I'd do besides get married. No one has talked about college to me, and Tim has flunked out.

Tim worked at one of the factories this past summer. There's a chance he could get laid off now. If that happens, he'll go to work in one of his dad's department stores.

After we're married, I dream of us living in this little apartment. I can picture Sunday afternoons. Tim will watch football on TV and drink a couple of beers. I'll be in the kitchen making doughnuts from scratch. I won't even mind if he sits around in his t-shirt.

This summer Tim's mom, Mrs. Larsen, hires me to clean her house three days a week when her cleaning lady is off. At first I like the job. I love making Tim's bed, smelling his sheets and being in his room. Most days, Mrs. Larsen goes to the Country Club while I clean. I turn on music and sing while I work. Toward the end of the summer, Mrs. Larsen starts criticizing everything I do. Then one day she tells me to clean the wooden library floor between the cracks with a knife. I'm thinking she wants me to work cleaning house so I'll hate housework and decide not to get married. I do end up hating to clean her place. I think it'll be different when I have my own place to clean.

Mom and Dad were divorced this summer. I don't know exactly what day it happened. It was near the end of July. Dad is still bitching about having to pay Mom nearly a half a million dollars. Dad got everything else. He got custody of Gordie and me. He got the house and all the furniture. I keep wondering how Mom lives. I haven't heard from her at all. Dad says she has a nice apartment and he bought her all new furniture. I'll never end up divorced, that's for sure.

Why hasn't Mom ever called or visited Gordie and me? Her feelings are probably hurt because we stayed with Dad. Gordie feels worse about not seeing Mom than I do. He told her that if she really loved him, she'd quit drinking. He can't forget that she wouldn't do it for him.

* * *

Gordie and I had decided to let the social worker pick who

we should live with. We found out a few days before she
was coming that she wanted to talk to us alone. Right up
until the day she came we were still hoping she'd be able to
change things, like stop the drinking and the divorce.

What a disappointment the social worker was! Gordie and
I were all dressed up. Dad borrowed the neighbor's cleaning lady to clean the house and serve tea. I miss Eloise.

We're watching TV in the family room when we hear the
doorbell ring. We turn off the TV and race to the foyer.
We slow down to a walk so that the social worker won't
know how happy we are that she's here.

I can tell something is wrong with the lady as soon as we
take her into the living room. She keeps staring around,
with her mouth kind of open, looking dumb. She looks at
the three sofas and five chairs like she doesn't know where
to sit. I have to ask her if she wants to sit on one of the
loveseats by the fireplace. Gordie and I sit on the one
across from her. It might have been all right except Gigi
jumps up on her lap. She tells us to get the dog down.
She says she doesn't like dogs. That does it for Gordie and
me. Anyone that hates dogs hates kids too!

All she does is ask us a lot of dumb questions. She wants
to know if we love our dad and if we think he loves us.
Every kid loves his parents. How stupid to ask! Gigi keeps
trying to get close to her and smell her. She keeps trying to
keep the dog away. Gordie and I think it's funny. Poor
Gigi. All she wants to do is make friends. Gigi can't tell
when someone hates her.

The borrowed cleaning lady brings in tea and cookies on
the silver tea tray. She sits it on the low marble coffee table

between the two loveseats. That's a mistake, because Gigi
tries to eat a cookie. I can tell it shocks the social worker.
The cleaning lady can see that she hates Gigi, so she picks
the dog up and takes her in the kitchen. I still crack up
when I remember what Gordie does next. The social
worker is about to take a sip of tea when Gordie says, "Uh,
wait a minute." He gets up and goes over to her. He puts
his finger and thumb into her teacup and pretends to pull
out a dog hair. This social worker is so dumb she doesn't
know that poodles don't shed! The rest of the time she's
here, she doesn't touch her tea. Gigi is whining in the
kitchen.

I always thought social workers were brave people. This
one was afraid of dogs. I'd make a better social worker
than she is.

* * *

Only one other important fact happens all summer. I'm
supposed to testify in court about the accident that happened
when I was fifteen—when my forehead was smashed. We
go to court about whose fault the accident was. Dad says a
lot of witnesses are going to testify that the truck was
speeding. Dad wants me to swear that Mom stopped.
Mom doesn't show up for the trial. Dad says it will ruin
our lives if I don't say Mom stopped. I'm upset. I know
Mom didn't stop. Dad says I better tell the truth, that she
stopped at the stop sign. Dad tells me I'm very confused.

The strange part is that I can't remember anything that
happened in that courtroom. It's like I fainted. I remember
being out in the hall with Dad. I don't remember anything
after that. I don't know if I said anything. I don't even
know if I went into the courtroom. I know they decided it

was the truck driver's fault. It's the weirdest thing not being able to remember. I keep trying to, but I can't.

I could be crazy.

* * *

"Crissy, are you going to answer?" It's my civics teacher asking me a question. Suddenly I remember I'm in class.

"Tell us what you know about the John Birch Society. The class is waiting," he says.

I must've daydreamed through the whole class, staring at my ring.

"The John Birch Society is on the far right wing," I answer, hoping that's enough. That's all I remember from the beginning of class.

The bell rings, saving me. I better pay more attention if I'm going to get through my senior year and get married.

The civics teacher stops me on the way out. "You weren't paying attention, were you?" he asks.

"No, I'm sorry," I answer.

"I'd like you to know that the John Birch Society would support slavery if it happened today," he says.

I wonder why he cares if I know that. I wonder why I'd care to know that.

"You'll be voting some day. You'll need some knowledge

on which to base your decisions," he says as he dismisses me.

I walk to my psychology class thinking about what china pattern to pick for my everyday dishes. Still, I try to figure out what the John Birch Society has against colored people. They must be prejudiced. I think about Eloise.

* * *

The psychology teacher says I'm supposed to go see Mrs. Clark, my guidance counselor, right away.

I bet I get another lecture about my grades. She wants me to graduate. Oh well, at least she never asks me why I'm not studying.

Mrs. Clark asks me to sit down as she shuts the door.

"Crissy, your grades are terrible," she starts.

"I know. I'll try harder."

"We've tried that. It hasn't worked. Now I want to place you in a special education class." She smiles without her eyes moving. She's waiting for my reaction.

All I can think is I'll be in with the dummies and messed-up kids. I must be stupid. Dad's always telling me I am. I asked him once what my I.Q. was. He laughed and said it was 70. I looked it up in a book. It means I'm a moron.

"Crissy, say something," Mrs. Clark insists.

"Something," I reply, not trying to be smart. I answer like an idiot.

"All right, here's how it's going to be," she says, starting on a big explanation of what I'm going to be doing.

I stare at my art class folder while she tells me I'm going to classes just in the morning. I'll be taking English For Every Day Living, a math class that teaches how to fill out bank deposits and stuff, and some class for my history requirement. In the afternoons I'm going to be working in a hardware store, if I pass an interview with the owner.

She ends her little talk with, "You must treat this as a real job. It's a wonderful opportunity and you'll be paid minimum wage. Isn't that nice?"

"Great," I whisper, hoping I can get out of her office now.

Mrs. Clark has more to say. She explains this will make it possible for me to graduate, and give me skills to get a job.

I make my only protest. "I'm getting married. I won't need a job."

"Yes, I've heard." She says it in a way I can tell she thinks I'm committing a sin.

I leave her office thinking about what I would do if I wasn't getting married. The only thing I can think of is becoming a call girl. I wonder how you start.

CHAPTER 23

November 23, 1964

Working at Verdon's Hardware stinks. It smells of paint and fertilizer. I dust toasters and help people find nuts and bolts. Boring! I never see any of my old friends at school. I never met any of the kids in my morning classes before.

At least there's a routine at home now. Dad does the shopping and I cook the dinners. Tim eats over almost every night, which is nice.

I've been experimenting with new recipes. Tonight I'm making "Chuckwagon Casserole." I found it in <u>Good Housekeeping</u> magazine. It says it's great for cold winter nights around the fire. Some dishes I've made have been delicious. Some have been pretty awful.

Tomorrow is Thanksgiving.

Last week I made spaghetti. The recipe calls for two whole cloves of garlic. I'm looking at the two garlic bulbs in the package. Each one is smaller than an onion. I figure if I chop them both up they'll equal one little bottle of Spice Island garlic. I pour the whole bottle into the sauce. I find out later that a clove is just one little piece of a bulb! It doesn't taste too bad, but the next day everyone at school says my breath is repulsive.

Two days later Susan says she can still smell it. She and I are friends again, though not as close as we used to be. She and Tim don't like each other that much. He doesn't even like the way she sits! She says I'm too young to get married. I hope they'll get along better once we are. Susan's going to stand up for me.

This chuckwagon casserole I'm making is a combination of corn, eggs, green olives and hotdogs. I'm chopping the olives. The oven is pre-heating. I wish I was making Thanksgiving dinner tomorrow. I've never cooked a turkey before.

When I ask Dad if we can have everyone here for Thanksgiving, he says no. I want to bug him about why we can't, but I don't want to push him too far. Everything is fairly peaceful right now. Tim and Dad are getting along okay. Dad catches us "doing it" one night in my room, and all he says to Tim is, "I think you better go home now," which Tim did. Dad isn't as mean as he used to be, since the divorce. He still drinks a bottle of vodka every night. Even Gordie's hands and feet are itching less. The problem now is he's got acne.

The reason I want to have Thanksgiving here is I want to invite Tim's parents. Tim is planning on coming with me to my grandparents' house. I don't want his parents to think they're being left out, but my grandparents didn't invite them.

One of the hard parts of cooking is making everything come out at the same time. I figure out the time for each dish and set the timer when the next one has to start cooking.

Bzzzz . . . time for the rolls to go in the oven. The casserole is supposed to cook for forty minutes. The rolls only take twelve. I've learned to pick foods that can be cooked at the same oven temperature.

The other hard part about cooking is getting everyone home on time. Gordie is always here, but mostly Dad is late. Tim is eating at his house tonight. His mom is making their Thanksgiving dinner now so he can be with me tomorrow.

The only thing no one can do in this kitchen is have the oven door open and open the door to the garage at the same time. Mom complained about it all the time when we first moved here.

I just get the oven door open and someone starts banging the garage door against it. It's Mom.

I don't know what to say or do. She's drunk. Dad is right behind her. Mom is trying to stand up and say hello to me.

I grab her by the arm so she doesn't fall against the hot oven.

"Help me get her upstairs," says Dad. He has that wild look in his eyes.

Dad and I get her into bed. She keeps saying, "Thank you, thank you."

We cover her up in Dad's bed and turn off the lights.

On the way downstairs, I ask Dad, "What's she doing here?"

"She's sick. Where else is she going to go?" he asks.

"She's drunk. You guys are divorced. She doesn't belong here anymore," I say.

"Look," Dad says, "she parked her car in a bad neighborhood. Someone took the tires off the rear end. She didn't notice it. She drove the goddamn car halfway down the street! Someone called the police. The car's still in my name, so they called me. I picked her up at the police station."

* * *

I burn the rolls just like Mom always did. The chuckwagon casserole is disgusting. I'll never mix eggs, olives and hotdogs again!

Thanksgiving Day

Dad says we all have to act normal for Thanksgiving dinner. We aren't allowed to tell that Mom's in our house.

Dad tells Tim, "I think you can understand this is a rather disturbing situation and it would ruin everyone's Thanksgiving."

Dad, Gordie and I ride over to Grandpa and Grandma's in Tim's car. Tim likes to drive.

Somehow, knowing Mom is home alone bothers me. It must be terrible to be alone at Thanksgiving while everyone else is over here at my grandparents. Mom must be thinking of all the times we were a family at Thanksgiving. She could've come, but I guess it would've been embarrassing for Dad.

There's not much for Tim and me to do before dinner. My cousins are all younger. The adults spend more time drinking before dinner than they ever do eating. At least there's tons of shrimp and dip to snack on.

We got here at noon. It's six o'clock when we sit down to eat. Usually, I eat loads at Thanksgiving, but something isn't right. Maybe I'm getting the flu. I finish heaping my plate and now I can't eat a bite.

Tim is sitting next to me. He's eating. Everyone is eating but me.

"Crissy, what's the matter?" asks my grandmother. "You haven't touched your plate."

"I don't know, Grandma. I feel sick all of a sudden," I answer.

Everyone stops talking and stares at me.

"It might help if you went and laid down on my bed for a while," says Grandma.

I don't know what makes me say, "No. I have to go home right away." I stand up and say to Tim, "Come on. Please take me home."

"You can't leave," says Dad. "Tim just started eating."

"I have to go home right now!" I insist.

"It's okay. I'll take her home," Tim says, as he shovels a big piece of turkey topped with mashed potatoes into his mouth.

"I said you couldn't leave," Dad hisses at me.

"Leave her alone, George," my grandma says.

"Come on Tim. I've got to get home," I say to Tim.

"We'll give your dad and Gordie a ride home," says my grandpa.

Tim and I say goodby quickly. I can tell Dad's going to be angry when he gets home, but I don't care.

"Why did you want to leave in such a hurry?" Tim asks when we get in the car. "Are you really sick?"

"I don't know. I've got this feeling I have to get home. Right now!" I answer. My voice is shaky.

Tim looks at me like I'm crazy.

It's the strangest feeling. "I <u>know</u> I have to get home," I answer his look.

"Maybe you're upset because of your mom being home," Tim offers.

"I don't know." We ride the rest of the way without talking.

It's only ten minutes between my grandparents' house and our house. Tim parks in front. It's starting to snow. I'm feeling odd because I wanted to leave so fast. I open the front door.

"Do you want a Coke?" I ask Tim. "I'm sorry I didn't let you finish your dinner."

"That's okay. We can catch the rest of the football game. I'll fix Cokes. Go turn on channel seven," says Tim.

The house is quiet. I walk through the downstairs rooms looking for Mom. All the lights are on, but the rooms are empty. It looks like a hundred people should be here. I can't even find one.

I leave Tim in the kitchen. He's pulling out ice cube trays. They're all empty.

All the lights are on upstairs too. I turn on the TV and look in the other bedrooms. Either Mom has left, or she's passed out in the basement. I start downstairs to look when I hear Tim yelling.

"Crissy! Come quick! Hurry up! Call 911!" Tim sounds panicky.

I run down the stairs, into the kitchen. The door to the garage is open. I get to the door in time to watch Tim dragging Mom out of Dad's car. She's slumped over like she's passed out.

"Crissy, call 911! Right now!" Tim's face is red. Mom's face is kinda pink and red too.

It's a minute before I can move.

"Crissy, your mom's trying to kill herself!" Tim's screaming at me again.

I dial 911 from the kitchen wall phone. I tell them my mom's trying to kill herself with carbon monoxide poisoning. The lady on the other end is very calm.

"Someone will be right there, honey," says the lady at 911.

Tim's carrying Mom into the kitchen.

"Crissy, push the garage door button. We've got to get the door open," he's shouting.

The garage door grinds open. Tim is half dragging Mom down the hall to the family room. I close the kitchen door so no more car fumes will get into the house. Tim already turned the car off.

I can't believe this. It's Thanksgiving. We're all having a nice dinner and Mom is home killing herself. She's just sitting in the car in the garage. Waiting.

Tim has Mom lying on one of the Moroccan rugs in the family room. He's sweating from carrying her.

"I better call Dad," I say.

"Did the Rescue Squad say how long it'll take?" he asks.

"They said right away. Is she still alive?"

"I think so. I can't tell."

"We should feel her pulse. Aren't we supposed to do something?" I ask Tim.

"I don't know. Call your dad."

Grandma answers the phone. I say, "Let me speak to Dad right away."

"Crissy, are you all right? You looked so pale when you left," Grandma asks.

"Grandma, please, it's an emergency!" I beg.

"All right." Grandma sounds hurt because I won't tell her what's wrong.

"What going on?" Dad asks.

"Mom tried to kill herself by turning on the car in the garage."

"I'll be right there." Dad hangs up the phone.

The paramedics are at the door. As soon as I open it, three of them rush past me.

"She's in the family room. That way." I point them to the hallway at the end of the foyer.

Tim puts his arm around me as we watch the paramedics. They're opening cases and putting a mask on her face.

One of them walks over to us.

"Are you the one that called?" he asks.

I nod my head yes. "She's my mother."

The paramedics are still asking Tim and me everything that happened when Dad and Grandpa come into the room. The other two paramedics are still working over Mom.

"Is she going to be all right?" he asks them.

One of them answers, "She's alive."

Dad tells us to leave the room. One of the other paramedics says, "If it weren't for these kids, she'd be dead."

"I think it's better if they go in the kitchen," Dad commands.

I'm kinda relieved, except I want to see how Mom's going to turn out.

Tim and I wait almost an hour sitting at the kitchen table watching the clock. I'm proud of what Tim did.

"How did you know she was in the garage?" I ask.

"I thought I smelled something. I couldn't figure out what it was. Then I heard the car running." He shakes his head like he can't believe it.

"You probably saved her life."

"It's funny, Crissy. If you hadn't wanted to leave your grandparents' house, I wouldn't have found her in time."

The rest of the time we sit silently, trying to hear what's going on in the family room.

Finally I can't stand it anymore. "Tim, I'm going back in there."

"Your dad will get mad."

"I don't care," I say, getting up.

Mom still has an oxygen mask over her face. Her back is leaning against Dad's green leather recliner.

Dad's arguing with the paramedics. He says he isn't going to let her go to the hospital. He says we'll take care of her.

The rescue man is saying that Mom should be in the hospital where they can run some tests and watch her.

"Dad, let her go!" I beg him.

"Young lady, you stay out of this! I don't need the whole world knowing!"

My grandfather agrees with him. "There's been enough trouble without involving more people," Grandpa adds.

I can't believe it! One more time they're going to pretend like nothing's happened!

The Rescue Squad leaves, saying they won't be responsible if something goes wrong.

Dad tells Tim to go home. My grandpa says Gordie can spend the night at his house, and he leaves. Dad never thanks Tim or me for anything we did.

Dad makes me help him get Mom up to bed.

So here I am with Mom and Dad.

* * *

No one ever mentions that Thanksgiving day again in my family. Tim is the only one I can talk to about it. I tried talking to Dad about it once. He says, "It was just an accident."

Everyone pretends like Mom didn't want to kill herself.

I keep wondering how I knew I had to come home in the middle of Thanksgiving dinner. I keep thinking we might be better off if Mom had died. She drank all the rest of that weekend. There was no sense talking to her.

Some people say suicide is a sin. I wonder if people who want to die should be allowed to?

Dad never says a word about Mom. Monday, when I come home from school, she's gone.

CHAPTER 24

May 3, 1965

There are tricks I use to get rid of bad thoughts. They are ways of forgetting terrible times. One of the tricks I use is thinking about swimming. It's weird. I used to watch my parents beating each other up, and all the time I'd think about swimming. The words "I'm going swimming, I'm going swimming," come into my head. Then I think only about swimming. I tell myself it's silly, but it helps me forget.

The swimming trick must come from when I was little. All those summers I spent at Strawberry Lake when I was happy. I swam all day long. I'd dive deep. I'd dive until there was nothing except little streaks of sunlight to help me find my way back to the top. I'd go down to the darkest, coldest water. It scared me to go that deep, where there was nothing to hear but my heartbeat.

The older I get, the less the swimming wish works for me.

Another trick I use is to cuss. I swear until the bad memories and hurt are gone. I don't say the words out loud. I think them in my head.

Mom's suicide attempt is one of those things I want to forget. Whenever it comes to mind, I keep repeating, "Go to Hell!" or "Fuck you!" The problem is I can't swear that Thanksgiving day away completely. It stays in my mind. I keep seeing how she looked with the paramedics working over her. I think of how she almost died. She really wants to. I know that.

It's almost like she did. I haven't seen or heard from her since that weekend.

My newest way to forget is masturbation. I discover it one night by accident. Tim goes home after we make love. I'm lying in bed touching myself and half dreaming. I don't know how I find the right place. I rub myself in a way that feels super good. It's practically a miracle what happens. My body is out of control. It's shaking all over like a giant tickle.

I'm happy! I'm excited! It's my first climax! I call Tim as soon as I'm sure he's home. "I had a climax!"

Tim sounds irritated. I try to tell him it was more than nice. I want him to know it's the most wonderful moment of my life. Why is he angry? He says he's tired. I can't believe he isn't excited about my climax.

Now I masturbate all the time.

I'm reading about sex, too. At first I'm embarrassed checking out all the sex books in the library, but no one says anything. I feel like a sex maniac.

Not one book describes what a climax _feels_ like. One of the books describes epileptic seizures though. There are two kinds. One is "petite mal," a little seizure where the body doesn't shake. The other one is a "grand mal" seizure. That's when the body shakes all over. That's how I rate my climaxes. My petite mal climax is where someone else can be in the same room while I'm doing it under a blanket. They don't know what I'm doing because I stay still. My grand mal climaxes are much better. I make noises too.

I don't see how masturbating can hurt me. It takes my mind off my troubles.

I try to get Tim to touch me in the right way. I would like it if he could make me come. He won't even talk about it.

Now, whenever I think of Mom dying, the divorce, or all the drinking, I masturbate. It's great for forgetting things that hurt.

* * *

I ask Susan if she masturbates. She acts like it's bad. She says I think about sex too much. She says I'm going to get pregnant if Tim and I don't use birth control. She says withdrawal isn't good. It's working fine for us.

I think Susan is telling other people that Tim and I go all the way. Suddenly my other girlfriends are asking me about sex. They act like I know everything. A couple of them even say they know Tim and I are doing it. Susan is the only one who's supposed to know. I always deny it.

Susan is going to be my maid-of-honor. We're getting

along better than we used to, but not that well. Tim is fixing her up with a couple of blind dates.

I want to ask Susan if she told everyone about Tim and me, but I don't want to start a fight. She starts fights with me all the time.

This past weekend Tim fixes her up with a date with Gary Morris. She gets drunk at the party. I tell her she's trying to be like a guy by drinking so much. I know a lot of girls get drunk, but Susan does it every single time we go out. I ask her not to drink. She just gets mad.

Susan says I have a problem about drinking because of my mom. I <u>do</u> think it's worse for a girl to drink than a guy. She says her getting drunk is better than me going all the way and getting married at seventeen.

I'm hoping Susan will meet some guy who likes her. Maybe she'll stop getting drunk at every party.

She makes me think of Mom.

* * *

I hope Susan and I can get along until my wedding. It's only eight weeks away. This winter went fast. Tim is working for my dad. I'm getting all A's from the hardware store. It's funny getting graded by a store! Even my class grades are better. I'm pulling my grade point average up enough to graduate.

Studying has been easier this year. With Mom gone there aren't any fights.

My little brother is the one I worry about. I feel guilty getting married and leaving him alone with Dad. Dad just sits there getting drunk every night, same as always. He's been letting Gordie drink beer and read <u>Playboy</u> magazine before he goes to sleep. I wonder who's going to cook their dinner when I'm gone.

CHAPTER 25

May 20, 1965

Today I'm going to pick out my wedding gown. Susan is going with me. My grandmother and Tim's mom are taking us.

There's a part of me that wishes someone would tell me I can't get married. I wish they'd tell me I have to go to college first.

If I had a normal life I wouldn't be getting married. If I had a normal mother she'd stop me. This is one of those days I miss having a mother. It should be my mom going with me today. I get jealous of Susan and her mom. They fight, but they do things together.

I'm lying in bed thinking about the energy it takes to get up. I masturbate three times to take my mind off Mom. It makes me feel better. I'm still ready on time when Grandma comes to pick me up.

* * *

Trying on wedding gowns is hard work. The dresses are itchy and heavy. I look stupid and fat. This winter I gained back all the weight I lost, and more. I weigh a hundred and thirty-four pounds. This is ten pounds more than I weighed when I got mono.

It's not until I try on about twenty dresses that I find one. I look okay in it. It's lovely. There are little beads of crystal and pearl all over it. It has a long train that can be tucked up for dancing.

Susan says I look great in it. Mrs. Larsen and Grandma like it. Grandma doesn't say anything about how much it costs. She laughs and says, "Crissy has good taste."

Mrs. Larsen says the groom and ushers will have to wear tails to go with the dress. Mrs. Larsen is planning a lot of the wedding with my dad.

After trying on gowns, I want to go home and masturbate.

No one tells me that we're going to the Larsen's Country Club for dinner. My dad, Mr. Larsen and Tim are meeting us there. I would've liked it if they'd told me first.

I want to ask Grandma if I can just go home. We're in the bathroom of the bridal shop, alone. Susan is looking at bridesmaid dresses with Mrs. Larsen.

"Grandma, I hope you won't think it bad of me to ask, but . . ." I start to say when she interrupts me.

"Crissy, I want you to know you can ask me anything. I'm going to be just like your mom for you. I'm not up on all the . . ." She pauses, and her face turns red.

I realize she thinks I'm going to ask her about sex. I can tell she's very uncomfortable.

"That's okay, Grandma, I learned everything at school," I say. They really only showed us one movie on the curse, but I know she doesn't want to talk about it.

"Well, that's good. I know the world is changing," says Grandma as she moves quickly out of the restroom.

* * *

Dinner is a shocker. Mr. and Mrs. Larsen were keeping a few surprises for Tim and me.

At first Dad and Mrs. Larsen talk about the food for the wedding. Dad says the reception will be at our club, the Hill and Dale Country Club. He went there today and picked out the menu. It's going to be lobster, prime rib, and veal cordon bleu. They discuss the band. They say the band can play anything.

I wonder if Tim ever gets mad that they're planning everything.

There's going to be an open bar.

Susan keeps saying how wonderful the wedding sounds.

Mr. Larsen and Dad talk about how lucky we "kids" are. They talk about how they had to struggle so much. Grandma talks about how different things were when she was growing up in Scotland. Tim and I hardly talk at all. I want to leave after I finish my steak. Everybody is making a big deal that the best part of the dinner is yet to come. I'm worried that Dad is getting too drunk.

The waiter removes everyone's plates and Mr. Larsen orders two bottles of champagne for dessert. No one ever asks for identification at a country club, so the waiter pours a glass for Susan, Tim and me. Mr. Larsen calls for a toast.

Then he pulls some papers out of his inside pocket.

"Here's to your new home. We put a down payment on a great colonial for you," he says with a grin.

He hands the papers to Tim.

"It's a beautiful four bedroom colonial right on Shady Lake. It's our wedding gift," says Mrs. Larsen. I spill my champagne.

Mr. Larsen is lighting a cigar and smiling.

"Crissy, say something!" Susan nudges me.

"I can't believe it," I say.

Tim says, "Thank you very much."

They say we're going to drive over to see the house—right after one more little surprise.

Mr. Larsen reaches into his coat pocket again and pulls out airline tickets. "Another present! A honeymoon in Europe!" He winks and waves the tickets.

Susan leans over and whispers, "They must be really rich!"

This time it's my grandmother who asks if the cat's got my tongue.

All I can say is, "Thank you."

Tim says he can't believe it.

They all look so happy. I want to talk to Tim alone. Everyone is laughing and talking except Tim and me. Tim says we should go see the house. He asks for directions. Mr. Larsen insists we all leave together.

We are all waiting outside the country club while the doorman is getting the cars. Mr. Larsen tells me to close my eyes. I do. All I can hear is one of the cars driving up.

"Open your eyes, Crissy," says Mr. Larsen.

I do. There's a new, bright red mustang convertible. Mr. Larsen says it's another wedding gift. It's mine.

I'd never thought about what kind of car I'd buy if I had the money.

I don't know what to say.

"I love it," I stutter.

I <u>do</u> love it. I hope I'm acting happy enough to please everyone.

* * *

The house is very nice. It's bigger than I think we need.

Four bedrooms, a family room, kitchen nook, living room and dining room. It's already decorated with wallpaper and curtains.

It's all pretty hard to believe.

CHAPTER 26

August 21, 1965

Tim and I get married the week after I graduate from Farfield Hills High.

The wedding turns out okay.

Three days before the wedding Tim tells me he doesn't want to get married. That hurts. I almost cry in front of him. I feel the same way, but I've never told him. I thought telling him would hurt his feelings. Besides, it's too late to do anything. We've already opened all our presents. They're on display in the dining room at Dad's house. Plus, we've moved some stuff into our house.

At the wedding rehearsal, the minister gets mad at me for laughing. He says if I giggle during the real ceremony, he won't marry us.

Dad gets drunk at the reception. My little brother gets drunk at the reception. Tim's parents get drunk. Susan is drunk, too. Only Mom isn't there.

Dad and Gordie get into a fist fight. I don't see it happen. They're in the men's locker room. Gordie ends up with a black eye.

Susan falls over backwards trying to catch my bouquet.

Everyone says it's a great wedding.

* * *

The honeymoon in Portugal and Spain isn't what I expect. The first night we stay in a converted castle in Sintra, Portugal. I keep using the wrong silverware. Every time I do, the waiter replaces the piece. We use room service a lot.

The first night I have to get up to go to the bathroom. I can't figure out how to flush the toilet. I don't see the chain hanging from the ceiling. It smells like an outhouse in the morning.

I feel tired and out of place the whole trip. I think people are staring at us because we look too young to be married.

The strange part of the honeymoon is how much I want to go home. I'm really homesick. I tell myself that my home was awful and Mom is gone. I reason there's nothing to miss at home. I think I miss my dog. I keep thinking about Gigi and Gordie.

I always thought I'd feel a million times better once I left home. I don't.

Dad and Tim's parents pick us up at O'Hare Airport. My ears are still clogged from the plane ride. I can't hear what everyone's saying, but I can tell they have a surprise for Tim and me. I dread it!

They drive us to our new house. The surprise is that they furnished the house and put our wedding gifts away. Dishes are in the cupboards. The refrigerator and freezer are stuffed with food. Everything is all done for us. I can't help thinking of that little apartment I wanted.

* * *

Tim gets up the next day and goes to work for his dad. There's nothing for me to do.

I'm angry that everything's done. I wanted to fix up my own house. Today I'm lying in bed. I'm bored. I could write thank you notes, but I don't want to. I hate writing because I can't spell.

I must be a very ungrateful person!

CHAPTER 27

February 17, 1966

It doesn't seem possible that Tim and I have already been married for seven months. I'm eighteen. I'm too young to be married. I think it's as if my life is under water. I keep trying to forget how it was at home. Bad memories are like air bubbles floating in water toward the surface. I wish I could go back to being a child.

I think I never was one.

I spend most of my days in bed, watching TV, dreaming of life. Some days I do nothing, not even answer the phone. Maybe I'll be a late bloomer, like Grandma says.

All our friends are in college. They drive home on weekends. Tim and I have a party every Friday and Saturday in our house. They come here because it's a place they can drink. I clean the house. I buy the food. They bring the booze. At most of the parties I go to sleep in the middle.

In the morning I get up early. It's me who cleans the white kitchen floor. It's covered with crumbs, spilt drinks and black heel marks. I go around picking up plates and ashtrays and glasses. I'm trying to lose weight so I fix a Tab for myself and scrub the floor with S.O.S.

Most of the time I'm too sick to get out of bed. The doctor can't find anything wrong with me. He says it's all in my head.

I have no energy. Sometimes I get dizzy when I stand up. I feel faint just going to the bathroom.

Tim says I'm lazy.

* * *

Christmas is awful this year. We have Christmas Eve dinner at our house. Dad is drunk when he arrives. He brings a twenty pound frozen ham. He hands it to me in a paper bag. The bag tears. The ham falls on my big toe and breaks it. I try to be polite in front of everyone. I hate complaining when I hurt.

I don't go to the doctor until the day after Christmas. All the doctor does is send me to the shoe repair shop. The repairman cuts the toe out of my shoe and puts a piece of wood on the bottom. This way my broken toe won't hit the ground. I try and not think of how it hurts!

Now, two days after New Year's, Dad calls. He never says he's sorry about my toe. Instead, he wants to talk about Mom. He hasn't mentioned her in over a year.

He says Mom married the guy she left with. His name is Jack Dievers. Dad has known she's been married for over a year. He says he didn't want to upset me by telling me. Now I have a stepfather I've never met. Great. I'm having a hard time adjusting to that fact. I can't imagine who'd marry Mom, as sick as she is.

Dad is still paying off the half a million dollars he owes Mom from the divorce. He says that's the only reason this Dievers guy married her. He married her for her money.

I'm wondering why Dad is telling me all this now.

"Crissy, your mother is in Memorial Hospital. She's in bad shape," he says. "She's in critical condition."

"Do you mean she's going to die?" I ask.

"I don't know. But she's your mother. I think you should go see her," Dad answers.

Dad explains that he doesn't think it would look right for him to go. He says Gordie has refused to go too.

Dad says the reason that Mom is in the hospital is because my new stepfather beat her up. One minute I find out I have a stepfather and the next minute I find he's killing my mom. She's always trying to find ways to get herself killed.

It takes me all morning to get dressed. I practice walking so Mom won't know I have a broken toe. I don't want her to know I'm hurting.

* * *

At the hospital, I head straight for the information desk. The lady says they have no record of Mom. I start to leave when I remember that she's remarried. I ask the lady to look for a Wanda Dievers.

"Yes, here she is. Wanda Dievers. Intensive care. You can only visit her for ten minutes once every hour," the lady says. She gives me a card and tells me to follow the red arrows on the second floor.

The arrows point to a glass door. Inside is a big, round desk. All around the room are beds and machines. Each bed is separated from the other beds by yellow curtains. I can see all the beds at once. No one in the beds can see each other. I count six beds before the nurse comes.

I tell her who I want to see. She wants to know if I'm "immediate family." I tell her she's my mother.

"All right, but you can only stay ten minutes," she says. She hurries off to one of the beds where a bunch of doctors and nurses are working over an old man.

I've forgotten to ask her which bed is my mother's. I walk from one bed to the next, looking. I can't find her. Four of the six beds have men in them. That leaves just two beds with women. I walk back to one of them. I don't think it can be my mother because this lady is old and gray. Mom's only thirty-eight. She had me when she was twenty.

I walk to the other woman's bed. The woman has dark hair with some gray. Mom's hair is blonde. Plus, this woman doesn't look anything like Mom. She looks like a bag lady. There must be some mistake.

The woman feels me looking at her. She opens her eyes— those eyes that could kill me with a look.

It's Mom!

I can't believe how terrible she looks. If it weren't for her eyes I wouldn't know it was her. Her jaw is wired shut. I can tell she recognizes me. It looks like she's trying to smile. I hope my face doesn't show how awful I think she looks.

I look into her eyes, those eyes that can love or hate. She always did have the most incredible eyes!

She pats the bed next to her. I'm afraid I'm going to faint. She keeps on staring and staring, without blinking. I ask her if I can get her anything. She keeps on staring.

I think she's trying to say I love you with her eyes.

Ten minutes has never been so long. Finally the nurse tells me it's time to leave.

"Goodbye, Mom," I say.

Her face is puffed out. Her eyes are purple. She keeps staring.

Out in the hospital hall I start to shake. I ask the nurse if Mom is going to be okay. She says I'll have to ask the doctor. I don't know who her doctor is.

I sit in the car for a long time before I feel calm enough to drive. Not being able to recognize your own mother is sad. I barely know her last name!

* * *

I call Dad to tell him about Mom. Gordie answers the phone. I start to tell him how bad Mom looks. He stops me from saying a word about her.

"My mother is dead. I never want to talk about her again," he says real loud.

He says Dad is too drunk to talk to me.

I know I'll never have the courage to go back to the hospital. I'm afraid if I go back, I'll run into my stepfather. I don't want to meet him. I never want to see my mom hurt that much again.

Maybe Mom won't die.

I can't sleep tonight.

February 22, 1985

If I die at this very moment, which is not unlike-y, I want everyone to know that I made up and changed all the times, places and names. I wanted to tell my story without hurting anyone. Just the same, this is my story. It really happened.

I'm in a small airplane flying between Skagway and Juneau in Southeast Alaska. The visibility is marginal. The pilot of this single engine plane is hanging close to the mountains. There are times when we see no land. The ride is bumpy. Sleet pelts the windshield. I'm trying to think of anything except this ride.

My job as an alcohol educator takes me all over Alaska. As my workshop finished today, I told the people about the end of my parents' lives.

Mom's death was slow. The man she married, Jack Dievers in the story, died in the bathroom. They were living in a rooming house. Afterward, Mom sat in a chair unable to move for three days.

People broke down the door when the smell of death became overpowering.

Mom was put in a nursing home. She was 39 years old.
The few times I went to see her, all she could do was echo
"Hello, hello, hello," over and over. She was confined to
her bed or wheelchair. She smiled at me through broken
teeth.

Alcohol had wasted her brain.

Dad died. His funeral was beautiful on a crispy winter day.
I rode in the back of a black limousine with his pretty
young widow. Yes, he married again. I don't know why she
stayed with him.

He drank until his liver swelled to great proportions. None
of my family has ever been near normal weight. I joke that
I come from a herd of hippos. Dad was biggest of all when
he had cirrhosis. He was 5 feet 10 inches and weighed
three hundred and ten pounds! He <u>did</u> stop drinking, but
it was too late.

Funny thing is, Dad died of ear cancer. Mom died 91 days
later of lung cancer. Neither one of their death certificates
listed alcoholism as the cause of death.

My first marriage did not last.

When my parents died I decided to get help. The first
psychologist I saw started me talking about my childhood.
I began to trust him after a few months. Then he commit-
ted suicide. It took awhile, but I got back into therapy
with another psychologist. He helped me find my true
feelings. He was excellent.

Now I live and travel the State of Alaska educating people
about the disease of alcoholism. I hope to reach as many

children of alcoholics as I can. One out of every five or six kids has an alcoholic parent just like me. I want every one of those kids to know they can grow up and be okay. Even if their parents don't get better. They don't have to keep it secret how much they hurt!

Still, there are times I wonder why I travel like this. Times I wonder why I sleep on classroom floors, ride snowgos, land on water and risk small plane rides like this one. Do people listen?

Two weeks ago my old friend, Susan in the story, died. She was alcoholic. She tried to stop drinking, and she tried Alcoholics Anonymous. But she didn't really want to stop, so she ran away to Florida. There she stumbled into a wooded area behind a 7-11 and slit her wrist. Her death certificate lists the cause of death as suicide. I know the truth.

The pilot of this little plane is sighing heavily. We're flying in an area of blind fog, no land in sight. Suddenly off to our left I see another plane. We're close to touching . . . to crashing! The other plane veers away just in time.

I meekly report seeing that plane to the pilot. He says he knows of no other plane in the area. But he'll check.

For a second I feel like a child. A child being told she's imagining something. I'm beginning to think, "Well, maybe the other plane wasn't really there." I don't say it.

Landing in Juneau, my legs are a bit shaky with leftover fear. I wait in line to put my baggage on the jet that will take me home to Anchorage. The pilot of the tiny plane approaches me. He says, "I want you to know you did see another plane. They had passengers. They were flying without a flight plan. That's very dangerous. I'm filing a report. The FAA will be calling you as a witness for the investigation." The bush pilot doesn't wait for my reply.

I feel satisfaction. Satisfaction in having been believed. I never felt that way as a child.

I head upstairs to the new airport restaurant and order hot tea with lemon and an Alaskan King Crab sandwich. Staring out at the Mendenhall Glacier, I wonder if it does any good to tell people my story when I teach classes on prevention of alcohol abuse.

* * *

The day after I learned Susan had died I called my brother. I think of him all the time. I told him about Susan's death and this book.

"What is it? A story about how horrible and mean Mom and Dad were to us?" His voice was belligerent.

"I hope not," I answered.

"Just remember, Mom and Dad also showed us a lot of love," he started flatly, and hung up.

The clouds are opening above the glacier.

My brother is right. Mom and Dad loved us a lot. That's why they stayed together for so long. At one time they were healthy, strong people. The last stages of alcoholism destroyed their feelings, bodies and spirits. Mom was sensitive and brilliant. Dad was staunch and passionate. They loved Gordie and me very much.

I don't want to bury anyone anymore. Not my family, not my friends. I don't want to pick up another Sunday paper and read how many died of drunk driving. <u>Not anymore!</u>

* * *

I think about the people who want to keep the things that matter in kids' lives out of the schools. Like alcohol and sexuality education. They say those values should be taught at home. They should see how those values were taught in my home. Besides, how can children learn anything at school when their home is a shambles? Right now there are an estimated 28 million children in alcoholic homes. They're living like I did.

It's like standing on a dangerous street corner watching the police and ambulance workers cleaning up accident . . . after accident . . . when what we need is a stoplight. Children of alcoholics need to learn about alcohol abuse prevention as soon as they can walk and talk. We need more pre-school programs.

* * *

The waitress serves my meal. The tea is steaming. There's plenty of lemon. My sandwich looks delicious. It's heaped with fresh crab with a little melted cheese on top. A few potato chips sit on the plate next to a pickle. Without thinking I munch on one of the chips. It's soggy with pickle juice. Yuck! I should know better than to eat potato chips!

My mind wanders back to the workshop I gave this morning. After I'd told my story, two teachers came up to me. One says, "Your story will change the way I think of alcoholics and their children. I'll treat them better." I smile remembering the wonderful teachers that helped me when I was little.

The other woman waits until we're alone. She takes a deep breath before she spills her secret, "My dad is an alcoholic."

She pauses. "Of course, my life was not as bad as yours."

"Oh?" I ask.

"Well, sometimes my dad would get drunk and chase me with a loaded gun," she replies.

"What did you do?" I ask her.

"I hid in the bathtub."

"What did you feel?"

Quickly she assures me, "Oh, I never took it seriously!"

We look each other in the eye and burst out laughing.

AN EPILOGUE—
PART II

Two years and eight months later... October 5, 1988

Write," says Maria Mack, my new editor.

"Write what?" I ask.

"Let people know what's happened to you. What you're doing today," urges the friendly voice of someone I've yet to meet.

October 22, 1988

For the past three weeks I've been traveling and writing.

I wrote from a motel overlooking the Kenai River in Alaska. I wrote on the plane to St. Louis. I typed page after page overlooking the stainless steel arch by the Missouri River.

I jotted notes in the air on my way to Portland.

Now I've finished. The icy blue view of Cook Inlet is visible from my room in the Anchorage Captain Cook Hotel.

* * *

When <u>Potato Chips for Breakfast</u> came out, my life started to change.

The words and pain were on paper never to be denied again. I thought. Some of my family found fault with the book. One aunt and uncle said it was okay if I wrote, but that I should call it fiction.

Was it fiction?

No. I remember it too clearly.

I challenged them to find something I'd said that wasn't true.

"That Thanksgiving when you said your mom tried to kill herself. She was calling your dad's bluff," they proposed.

"We could check. The paramedics must have kept records," I replied.

They had no answer for that.

* * *

My little brother is divorced. I hear he's married again. Our lives are different.

Word about my brother comes from my cousin Max. Gordie misses me. I miss him. He wants me to go back to visit. During that visit he wants me not to talk of bad things.

I can forgive, but I can't forget.

* * *

I order from room service: garlic soup, oysters, and shrimp.

I am forty-one years old. My oldest son, Tom, is steady, sturdy, and strong. He's in his second year of college and lives on campus. He'll soon be twenty. He is handsome and loyal. He's popular. He nurtures his friendships over distance and time. I'm proud of him.

He once told me that he wished I were like other mothers.

When he was ten, he asked me, "Mom, when I grow up, who am I gonna tell my children their grandfather is?" He wishes I hadn't been married four times.

Right after <u>Potato Chips for Breakfast</u> was published, my youngest son, Matt, asked to go live with his father in Denver. He was thirteen then. Too young, I thought, to be away from me.

My reaction was to take him to Herb Bischoff, a psychologist. The therapist saw him a few times. Then he offered to see me. See me! I'd had therapy. No, thank you, I didn't need any more. I went a few times for Matt's sake, and then I stopped going. But Dr. Bischoff kept after me. He'd call now and then to see how I was doing.

Finally, I worked through my anger at needing help. Dr. Bischoff worked on my resistance to counseling. Now, after almost two years, I can recall all of my childhood. I faced the sexual abuse I'd survived. I cannot speak of it publicly, yet.

Room service has arrived. A friend is here to share the feast. We sit on the floor and giggle and eat.

I've told all I can for today.

October 24, 1988

I heard on the radio this morning that there are three million homeless.

"Yeah, and I'm one of them," I told the radio.

If that isn't bad enough, my car is dead. It was to be expected. Old Betsy ran for eleven years and over 120,000 miles. She lasted longer than my longest marriage.

I've been told that one of the things I do best at my job is finding and stretching money. Today, I am determined to find a home and a new car. My lack of cash should be no obstacle.

I'm staying with one of my board members, Sharon Jean. She's good to me. Yesterday, she had lunch with my husband.

"If you two weren't so busy protecting each other's feelings, maybe you could get on with your lives," she said as a way of asking me why I'd left him.

How can I explain why I've left the man who helped me raise my children through their turbulent teens? Why I'm leaving the best marriage I've ever had?

This is the man who wasn't flustered when Tom, then sixteen, came home at five in the morning to report our truck was stuck in a Tonga forest. Tonga is a Russian word that means "drunken." The forest is aptly named because the trees tilt and list from side to side. The swampy land is unable to provide a solid foundation. All my husband said was that we were lucky it took only two tow trucks to get it out. He's been worried about having to hire a helicopter to do the job.

He was the one who gave me the freedom to cry on our sixth anniversary while out on a picture perfect lake. It was a bright, sunshiny Alaskan midnight. I cried because I'd gone through the pain of writing Potato Chips and could not find a publisher.

He was the man who brought me to Alaska, the one who started me writing and edited my rough drafts. He stood by me when my forgotten sexual abuse surfaced in my mind.

While I was in St. Louis for a convention, he was the one who helped my youngest son Matt pack and then put him on the plane to Denver to go and live with his real dad.

Matt said, "I love you, Mom, but I've been wanting to do this for a long time. Now that you and Pete are breaking up, it's time."

Matt said he'd been through enough pain. He said he'd be back to live with me for his junior and senior years. He is a tender soul.

Funny, I took Matt to counseling so he wouldn't leave. Now, my therapist says he made a good, adult decision.

He is a tender soul. He's artistic, bright, and charming. Last summer he took apart the engine of a car and put it back together in excellent running order.

He hates school and loves his job. He started as a dishwasher and in a matter of months became a cook. His self-esteem leaped forward.

I am very proud of both my sons. They are proud of me and my work.

My empty nest has come a little sooner than I'd expected.

So why did I leave home too?

October 25, 1988

Got a car. Good old Cal Worthington and his dog Spot, they were true to their advertising. I'm driving away in the first 1987 Pontiac Grand AM I tested. Not a bad deal. I have the car, I haven't put out a penny, and payments begin in December.

Getting a home. I head for a charming area downtown. There are winding streets and an inlet view that includes the mountain the natives call the Sleeping Lady. The first FOR RENT sign I stop at is on a bright, cheery place in Bootleggers Cove. The lady who owns it agrees not to cash my check until I say it's okay, and I can move in tomorrow. It's a few blocks from the lagoon, the new coastal trail, and three of my favorite restaurants.

The excitement of having my own place after weeks of hotels and staying with friends is soaring inside me.

I have never lived alone. I have spent twenty-two years married and raising my sons. One of my long-time friends from high school has written to express her happiness for me: "At last, Cindy, you're doing something for yourself. I can't tell you how happy I am for you."

I'm happy for me. My job as executive director of Planned Parenthood of Alaska allows me to fight for issues close to my heart. We have three medical clinics and a mobile clinic that travels the state, and we are in the process of opening our fourth clinic in Soldotna. I find myself enthusiastic as I fight for freedom of choice. It is becoming more difficult for women to have control over their body's reproductive health.

I don't want us to go back to the coat-hanger-abortion days of the sixties. Some people believe that taking the pill is an act of abortion. Abortion is a failure of some kind. For most there is grief involved, but an unplanned child's lifetime of grief is far worse. I pick up the paper and see pictures of starving children in overburdened countries of the world. It's not fair to suffer a lifetime of hunger.

My life is full. I have an excellent board of directors to guide me in my work and a wonderful staff to work with.

Yesterday, I told Dr. Bischoff that he'd be mentioned in my second epilogue. He said, "Yeah, you can tell them you're being kicked out of therapy."

"Not yet," I pleaded.

"No, you can still come back and work on any issue you're ready to work on. But, the biggest issue you have to work on now is terminating therapy." He smiled.

I was able to ask for a hug. I set my next appointment for around Thanksgiving. Holidays may always be hard for me.

There is a school of thought that believes the patient is ready to leave therapy when they've progressed into a healthy, loving relationship. I'm doing that now.

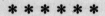

WHAT TO DO

Potato Chips for Breakfast is the autobiography of a young girl struggling to survive in the chaos of a family with two alcoholic parents. Most biographies and novels that touch on drinking behaviors make believe that they are about something other than alcoholism. This book doesn't make believe. It is a tense, unromantic work. Cynthia Scales ("Crissy" in the book) brings to the printed page the raw experience of tens of millions of us living in the United States today.

In the 1970's, there were an estimated 28 million children with one or more alcoholic parents living in the United States. Reports in the early 1980's estimated half a million school age children of alcoholics lived in New York State alone. In 1982, the Gallup poll found that 40% of young people between 18 and 24 had a family member with an alcohol problem.

When I was a young man growing up in the North Country of New York State, I didn't have an alcoholic parent. My brother and sister didn't have an alcoholic parent. None of the neighborhood kids I played with had an alcoholic parent. There was a St. Bernard that a local college fraternity plied with beer. He was often seen ambling toward a tavern frequented by students. Everybody in town knew that poor dog had a problem.

I had crazy, weird, angry, dangerous and insensitive parents. Sometimes they drank too much.

A few months before my 29th birthday, my mother phoned me to announce that she had found Alcoholics Anonymous. Until that moment, I had no idea that our family's craziness was due to alcoholism. But in that single instant, all my family's history became suddenly relevant. Yet, it was another year before I could speak the words "mother" and "alcoholic" in the same sentence without choking.

The facts of alcoholism and of our family's involvement in it had been denied to me and my brother and sister all our lives. Alcohol was never a subject taught in school. Any mention at any time, in any place, that drinking in my family might be out of the ordinary, was forbidden. The death of a colleague from cirrhosis might be whispered, but when a family member died from cirrhosis, we denied the cause and called it hepatitis. Driving while intoxicated was a joke. Everybody did it. Weddings and birthdays and funerals were celebrated by getting drunk. When the barn burned, the first thing my father did was buy a case of beer for the fire department. Wherever alcoholics were in my life, they set the norm. Alcoholic behavior was normal before I ever picked up a drink. I knew nothing else.

I'm not surprised that I knew nothing else. Children of alcoholics have been neglected and forgotten for centuries while everyone was busy noticing the alcoholics. The impetus for treatment of alcoholics and their children has only rarely originated with the professional community. As late as 1983, doctoral students complained to me that their universities did not think children of alcoholics a valid topic for study. Physicians, social workers, psychologists and teachers still beat their breasts, believing nothing can be done for the alcoholic. Unless he wants help, they say.

And unless the alcoholic gets help, they believe, nothing can be done for the children. Neither proposition is true.

After reading Potato Chips for Breakfast, it is hard to deny the realities in the life of Cynthia Scales and others like her. When denial is weakened, action becomes possible.

Reading between the lines and listening to the truth of the pain in Cynthia Scales' life, you will understand much of her behavior. Notice how Crissy avoids every feeling. It is the denial of reality, rather than the drinking itself, that causes so many behavior problems in the alcoholic family. Denial by every one of us: parents, siblings, teachers, doctors and friends. The conspiracy of silence that surrounds the alcoholic family leads to chronic details in the reality checking process and in the ability to recognize and express feelings. It is the silence of denial that is crazy-making!

This is my story, the story I never had the courage or the discipline to write. Inside each of us is the belief, itself a denial of reality, that it "wasn't that bad." It was that bad. The fact that the pain of alcoholism involves millions of children and their families numbs the mind and blurs the truth.

To listen to one child's pain is to accept your membership in the human race. Such acceptance does not imply acceptance of responsibility for the cause or cure of that pain. Nobody—not you, not me, not the alcoholic—is responsible for the alcoholism. The person who experiences the pain of alcoholism is only responsible for recovery from it. Nevertheless, it is my belief and hope that if you listen just once to the pain of any child affected by alcoholism in the family, you will never again remain silent. That is why Potato Chips for Breakfast is important. I believe that, after having read this book, you will not be able to maintain the silent denial that permits alcoholism to flourish.

I could write a lengthy essay showing why this autobiography in particular is an accurate portrayal of the alcoholic family. The proof, however, lies in the reading. Show this book to <u>any</u> child or adult who can read (and whom you might suspect on the flimsiest of evidence to have a problem of alcohol in the family). That child will come back to you and say. "This is how it is." And then you and that person can start discussing what the two of you together can do to start healing the pain.

One more thing. Most alcoholics don't get better. About 85% die directly from the disease or from its side-effects. But young people with an alcoholic parent don't have to wait for their parents to stop drinking in order to take charge of their own recovery. Cynthia Scales is a survivor, now recovering from her family's alcoholism. So am I. So are many of my friends. The knowledge that recovery from the chronic trauma of family alcoholism is necessary and possible is growing rapidly in every community in the United States. There are self-help groups for adult and teenage children of alcoholics in most areas of the country. Following are some suggestions about where to look for further information about children of alcoholics in your community.

If you are, like me, the child of an alcoholic, if you identify with most of the characterisitics of children of alcoholics listed at the end of this book, if you read <u>Potato Chips</u> and said, "Crissy is me," then reach out. We're here in the sunlight waiting for you.

Thomas W. Perrin, M.A.
Rutherford, New Jersey
January, 1986

Information and Referral Sources
for Children of Alcoholics

Prepared by Thomas W. Perrin

The easiest source of information about alcoholism is your local telephone book. Check the Yellow Pages under **Alcoholism Information and Treatment Centers.** Additional listings are often found in the White Pages under **Alcoholics** and under **National Council on Alcoholism** (or the name of your county or state).

Adult Children of Alcoholics, Inc., has information on self-help groups for adult children that are not affiliated with Al-Anon Family Groups. POB 3216, Torrance, CA 90505. (213) 534-1815.

Al-Anon Family Groups is the central source of information about self-help groups for teenage children of alcoholics (Alateen). Many hundreds of groups for adult children of alcoholics are also listed with Al-Anon. POB 182, Madison Square Station, New York, NY 10159.

Children of Alcoholics Foundation, Inc., has published several high quality reports about children of alcoholics. 200 Park Avenue, 31st Floor, New York, NY 10166.

COA Review, The Newsletter About Children of Alcoholics, contains resources, book reviews, and articles about children of alcoholics. COA REVIEW, POB 190, Rutherford NJ 07070.

Codependents Anonymous are self-help groups for adult men and women from dysfunctional (not necessarily alcoholic) families. POB 5508, Glendale, AZ 85312.

Humboldt A.C.A. World Service Committee is a networking service for adult children of alcoholics groups. POB 6225, Eureka, CA 95502. (707) 443-3836.

National Association for Children of Alcoholics (NACoA) is a national advocacy organization for children (of all ages) of alcoholics, with chapters in many states. 31582 Coast Highway, Suite B, South Laguna, CA 92677. (714) 499-3889.

National Clearinghouse for Alcohol Information provides a variety of bibliographic and other alcohol information services, some free, some at moderate cost. NCALI, POB 2345, Rockville, MD 20852. (301) 468-2600.

Perrin & Treggett annually publishes a bibliography of available books on children of alcoholics. Perrin & Treggett, POB 190, Rutherford, NJ 07070. 1-800-321-7912.

Substance Abuse Librarians and Information Specialists (SALIS) is a networking association, with a major focus on libraries, clearinghouses, information centers, and resource centers on alcohol and other drugs. SALIS, Alcohol Research Group, 1816 Scenic Ave, Berkeley, CA 94709. (415) 642-5208.

* * *

Bass, Ellen, and Laura Davis, *The Courage to Heal: A Guide for Women Survivors of Sexual Abuse* (Harper & Row, 1988).

Common Characteristics
of Adult Children from
Dysfunctional Families

The following statements are characteristic of adults who have grown up in alcoholic or abusive families. Although most people probably will identify with two or three of these statements, it is the children from severely dysfunctional families that identify with the majority of them.

1. I guess at what normal is.

2. I have difficulty following projects through from beginning to end.

3. I lie when it would be just as easy to tell the truth.

4. I judge myself without mercy.

5. I have difficulty having fun.

6. I take myself very seriously.

7. I have difficulty with intimate relationships.

8. I overreact to changes over which I have no control.

9. I feel different from other people.

10. I constantly seek approval and affirmation.

11. I am either super responsible or super irresponsible.

12. I am extremely loyal even in the face of evidence that the loyalty is undeserved.

13. I look for immediate as opposed to deferred gratification.

14. I lock myself into a course of action without giving serious consideration to alternate behaviors or possible consequences.

15. I seek tension and crisis and then complain about the results.

16. I avoid conflict or aggravate it; rarely do I deal with it.

17. I fear rejection and abandonment, yet I am rejecting of others.

18. I fear failure, but sabotage my success.

19. I fear criticism and judgment, yet I criticize and judge others.

20. I manage my time poorly and do not set my priorities in a way that works well for me.

ABOUT THE AUTHOR

Cindy Scales graduated from Metropolitan State College in Denver, CO with a Human Services Degree. During her first years in Alaska she was a Prevention Trainer for the Alaska Council on Prevention of Alcohol and Drug Abuse, traveling the state of Alaska offering workshops for teachers, parents, professionals and children. She has also appeared on numerous radio and television programs as well as participating in the filming of two alcohol abuse prevention films for young children which are used in programs across the nation. Currently, she is the Executive Director of Planned Parenthood of Alaska and the mother of two teenage sons.